DATE DUE

APR 0 3 2017		

Demco, Inc. 38-293

THE

Everyday

ENTREPRENEUR

THE

Everyday

ENTREPRENEUR

APPLY THE TRiPPLE THREAT

OF

AMBiTiON, CONFiDENCE, AND CONViCTiON

FOR

SUCCESS ON YOUR OWN TERMS

ROB BASSO

with Adina Genn

WILEY

John Wiley & Sons, Inc.

Published by John Wiley & Sons, Inc., Hoboken, New Jersey.

Published simultaneously in Canada.

For general information on our other products and services or for technical support, please contact our Customer Care Department within the United States at (800) 762-2974, outside the United States at (317) 572-3993 or fax (317) 572-4002.

Wiley publishes in a variety of print and electronic formats and by print-on-demand. Some material included with standard print versions of this book may not be included in e-books or in print-on-demand. If this book refers to media such as a CD or DVD that is not included in the version you purchased, you may download this material at http://booksupport.wiley.com. For more information about Wiley products, visit www.wiley.com.

Library of Congress Cataloging-in-Publication Data:

Basso, Rob.
   The everyday entrepreneur/Rob Basso. – 1st ed.
      p. cm.
Includes index.
  ISBN: 978-1-118-10644-0 (hardback)
  ISBN: 978-1-118-14996-6 (ebk)
  ISBN: 978-1-118-14997-3 (ebk)
  ISBN: 978-1-118-14995-9 (ebk)
  1.   Entrepreneurship. 2.   New business enterprises–Management. I.   Title.
  HB615.B386 2011
  658.1′1–dc23   2011022709

Printed in the United States of America

10 9 8 7 6 5 4 3 2 1

To my wife, Mary Beth, son Nicholas, and daughter Skylar

Contents

Foreword

ENTREPRENEURSHIP: IT'S NOT just an idea; it's a lifestyle. It's a decision, a mission that can only be accomplished by someone who displays a tremendous amount of focus, dedication, thoughtful planning, and above all, passion. Funny—I think I just described Rob Basso.

The first time I met Rob, we immediately started chatting about business. I thought it would just be a polite talk, high level at best, but boy was I wrong! Rob loves business and everything about it—the idea of it, the strategy, the people, and the intellectual challenges it presents. He has worked with countless business owners and entrepreneurs, and in this book he uses his vast knowledge base and experience to guide all of us through the turbulent waters of an ever-changing business landscape and into the safe harbors of success and realized dreams.

So what does it take to make it as an entrepreneur? How do we get to that promised land? Well, frankly, it starts with something simple—a dream. Entrepreneurs don't do what they do because it's merely a job or a living. They do it because they've found a wrong in the world that they truly believe they can right, or have discovered a gaping hole in the space between what exists today and what could exist tomorrow, and will never sleep again until they plug that hole. It starts with an idea that burns a hot flame deep inside you. And nothing can douse that flame except success.

An idea, however, is like a balloon drifting on the breeze. It's cool to look at, and it captures our attention, but without focus, a roadmap, and a plan, it slowly drifts away to an unknown destination. The difference between an idea's mere existence and its actual realization comes from a need to turn that flame burning inside of us into a *product*. That's where it all starts. The world's most successful entrepreneurs are the ones who can bridge that treacherous gap between a good idea and an actual business. And make no mistake—that process is hard. It's just plain difficult. Look around you. Almost everyone you know has a great idea that they're going to quit their worthless job someday. Aren't they all going to turn their amorphous flame of an idea into an actual profit-making company? Yeah, right. The reality is that if it were easy, everyone would do it. Because it's a challenge, very few do.

Yet somehow, some people actually do manage to transform their mere ideas into professional success. How? What are they doing differently from everyone else? Over the course of reading this book—and by way of examining everything else that Rob does—you're about to find out. Entrepreneurship is a journey, and it's one worth sharing. The reason that Rob and I found so much to talk about was because we had both been to the promised land of entrepreneurial success. We'd both started with a simple idea, turned it into a product, wrapped a company around that product, and then grew that company into a thriving, profitable business that created jobs for many people and value for its stakeholders. (Wow—don't forget to take pictures along the way!)

So now it's your turn. You have an idea, right? Maybe you've already started your business. But you want more. You want to turn something small into something big—something that costs money into something that makes money. Well—you can do it. Hey, even I did it, and I'm just a regular guy. However, I did a few things that helped me along the way. I paid attention. I studied what the winners did, and I learned from mistakes the losers made. I also discovered some things along the way that I'd like to share. In fact, I couldn't wait to communicate my own insights for this book when Rob told me that he was writing it. Rob let me know that he wanted to collect all the lessons that so many of us lived through and share them in a way that would help all of you potential entrepreneurs avoid the mistakes we made and benefit from the things we did right.

Entrepreneurs take risks. They try things that might not work, things they've never tried before, or the things they've tried before but in totally different ways the second (or third or fourth) time around. Over the years, I've observed that the best entrepreneurs have overcome their fear of failure and are far more afraid of *not trying* than of failing. As they see it, trying and failing is not the worst thing that can happen to you. Spending your whole life wondering what you might have achieved had you only tried is a far worse fate.

Smart entrepreneurs increase their odds of success with each try by collecting data and assimilating it into their overall plan and process. One of the most important pieces of data to collect is validation. Sure, you think your idea is the greatest idea ever. You're so sure of that fact that you've already picked out a yacht in *Boating World* magazine. And everyone around you thinks you're the smartest person they know and that your idea just can't fail. But therein lies the rub. Who are those people, anyway? Have they ever started with nothing more than a burning flame, a great idea, a driving passion, and then turned it into in an operating company with products, sales, service, and more? Maybe—in fact, probably—not.

So how do you validate your idea and make sure you're on the right path? The answer is to surround yourself with people who've been on this very path before, and who found a way to do it right. And then listen to them. Among other things that Rob and I have in common is the sheer delight we take in meeting successful people and learning about how they became successful. But Rob went a step further: He wrote this book. Thanks to him, you can use these pages to surround yourself with validation, with people who have been there before and have done it right.

My own entrepreneurial journey was one of trial and error. But I always got better. I started my first software company from scratch, and I later sold it to a Fortune 500 company for a very successful exit. I kept on creating ideas and launching companies, and I was even lucky enough to be part of the great Internet tidal wave when we launched Priceline.com, using the same principles I learned along the way, and that Rob has collected to share with you in this book. If I can do it, anyone can.

However, with that being said, I should emphasize that entrepreneurship isn't for everyone. It can be a life without security, a day without structure, a month without pay. But it can—and always will—be a life full of challenges. I, for one, wouldn't have it any other way. And neither would Rob. So we want you to jump in feet first and join us. Soak in the wisdom that Rob has gathered to share with you. I can't think of a better guy to write this book.

Oh, and don't forget to invite me to that yacht party! Something about the mystery of the sea fascinates me.

—Jeff Hoffman
**Cofounder and CEO in the
Priceline.com family of companies**

Acknowledgments

I⊤ TAKES A village to build something worthwhile; this book is certainly no exception.

Every entrepreneur I interviewed for this book has made it their mission to exceed expectations and take risks in order to find their calling. Then they took time out of their busy days to help you, my future reader, find success on your own terms, imparting their stories of joy and failures in the hope that you will live your own American dream.

I tend to throw myself into my projects and to need support from everyone around me in order to live my passion. Without the unwavering encouragement from my wife Mary Beth, son Nicholas, and daughter Skylar, this book and many other ventures would never have been possible. I hope I can return the favor as we build our lives together. Thanks and I love you.

My team at Advantage Payroll Services and Basso On Business, including Marty Lanz, Yvette Hector, Melissa Di Diego, Christine Cesarino, and Christina Federici, played a crucial role in providing the available time to complete this project. Longtime employees like Tina Singelton, Leadette Smith, Tony Hector, and the rest of the staff helped along the way. I could not ask for a better support team. They work hard every day to keep the ship sailing in the right direction. Thank you to each team member.

A special thank you is necessary for my friend Adam Schwam. His friendship and unwavering support for the projects I work on led me to meet Susan Spilka, a member of the John Wiley & Sons, Inc., team. Susan introduced me to the dedicated and hard working staff at Wiley who helped make this book possible.

Bill Corbett and Pete Cracovaner are my dream-team consultants that help guide my public relations, private coaching, and media career. They play an integral part in keeping me focused and on track for new and unforgettable journeys I have yet to take. Thanks for all your help.

My clients may not realize they played a role, but they did. I have spent the last 15 years building my businesses and I have met, and certainly will meet, many of the finest professionals that anyone could have the pleasure to work with. Their loyalty, patronage, and our relationships helped shape my outlook on life and business. Together we can help each other prosper and assist our fellow entrepreneurs and our communities. Thanks to each and every one of you.

Introduction

"PIPER FIVE GULF Tango, you are cleared for takeoff." Ground control was talking to me as I geared up for my first takeoff alone.

With wet palms, a racing heart, and sweat beading on my forehead, it dawned on me that my instructor was not next to me. My stomach churned, and I realized that there was no turning back.

As if on autopilot (no pun intended), I went through the motions I had done hundreds of times before with my instructor: I checked my lights, made sure I was on the proper heading, eased the throttle forward, checked the engine gauges one last time, rotated at 60 mph, and suddenly my little Piper Warrior plane was airborne.

"Speed up. You have Cablevision behind you." That was ground control again, and I heard the message loud and clear. You want to fly? Fly. Otherwise, move your ass, little guy, and stop playing around with the big guns.

This is where all the hours of training took over. Okay, so I was hardly in a league with New York's telecommunications and entertainment powerhouse Cablevision, but I could hold my own. Of this I was certain.

After a few touch-and-go moments, a series of required takeoffs and landings, it was all over, seemingly in the blink of an eye. I had just completed my first solo flight. I could actually fly an airplane—in the same airways as the corporate giants.

Had I just begun the ride of my life? Yes and no. When you manage a business—when you compete for the same clients and customers as the mega-players—you are constantly at the brink of takeoff or a rocky landing. But don't just take my word for it: Ask Jeff Hoffman, a cofounder of what ultimately became the flourishing travel search engine Priceline.com. Or talk to Joe Corcoran, who turned an off-Broadway interactive show, *Tony and Tina's Wedding*, into an international phenomenon. Like the other entrepreneurs I've interviewed for this book, these two know what it means to sweat in the pilot's seat. They understand this simple premise: When it comes to do-or-die decisions, the risk-taking comes down to you and you alone. But you wouldn't choose any other way.

On any given dark winter morning in the early 1980s, I used to hop on my bike knowing that at the ungodly hour of 5 AM, the only people I was likely to see in those suburban streets in South Jersey would be other newspaper boys like me. Most kids my age were still in their beds, grabbing their last hours of sleep before trudging off to school; however, delivering papers was the only option I knew. As the youngest of three boys and the product of working-class parents, I had to hit the pavement early if I wanted the kind of security that came with having some extra dollars in my pocket. Even as a 10-year-old kid, I was transfixed by the power of always earning an income. I realized even back then—in a world where life as you knew it could change in a heartbeat—that I could always rely on myself. Though I had not yet learned the word "entrepreneur," I was well on my way toward becoming one.

During those early-morning deliveries, sometimes in rain or snow, I had hours to go before I heard the bell ringing to signify the start of my traditional schooling. Yet I already knew that I was getting more lessons on that paper route than I would in most classrooms. I learned about taking risks—literally falling on my face, bouncing back, and winning loyalty. I learned about making something from absolutely nothing, and about believing in myself.

I know that I am not alone in this mind-set. Ask any everyday entrepreneur or millionaire next door about what made them strong enough to become the ultimate self-starter—to step ahead of the competition, convince others to have faith in them, and protect themselves from losing everything in the process—and you will see patterns emerge. Maybe these millionaires, too, had a paper route or a role model. Maybe they questioned authority early on and, because they were convincing, they won and continued to push against boundaries from that point on. These are the risk takers, the ones who are not afraid to expose themselves to possible failure, yet they find the confidence deep inside to carry them through.

The way in which we live with risk is a matter of personal preference. Some of us have a tendency to take risks into our personal lives, perhaps by flying small planes (or even jumping out of them). Some of us are cocky enough to flirt with millions of dollars of other people's money, or self-assured enough to get others to buy in as we trail blaze our way through some emerging trend. And that's what sets us apart from the rest.

You will meet some of these trailblazers in the pages of this book. Some of them are the original force behind now-familiar household brand names, including Priceline.com, TheaterMania .com, and Will Ferrell's *You're Welcome America*. Some have been tapped by the show *Project Runway* and Manhattan's famed Whitney Museum of American Art for unique perspectives that they were not afraid to express. Some made it in industries far less glamorous, but made it nonetheless. And just as it was with me, it was something in their formative years—that job, that moment of self-reliance—that enabled them to plow forward and become unstoppable on their way to the top.

One common thread is that none of us remained stagnant at any point. We plunged forward in our personal missions, whether it was to raise enough money to start a company or a production, or even simply to afford college tuition. Many of us began to define success by observing our parents' definition of it; in this way, we learned what to do—and maybe even more importantly, what not to do—in order to achieve it. We became dedicated as we paved our own way. We hit the pavement early, selling our wares

Entrepreneurial Insight

What do entrepreneurs have in common? The drive to advance. As a rule, this group of people does not let obstacles get in the way of moving forward, whether they need to raise money to get a venture going or they need to educate themselves about an industry, inside and out.

door-to-door, finding new markets, new possibilities, and new audiences. For me, success was a byproduct of moving onward. I was in constant motion. No lemonade stands for me; they were too static.

1

Lemonade Stands Are Just Too Static

Early Lessons

By definition, if you're willing to take risks, you are willing to take a hit, all in the name of the potential big win. There's an inner confidence that's practically a prerequisite to risk-taking—a belief that win or lose, you'll carry on, and maybe even become that much stronger for it.

As kids, we took great pains to fit in—at almost all costs, and even as we tried to push boundaries. But those of us willing to march to our own tunes, expose ourselves to the judgment of others, and convince people to try things our way—well, we were getting a jumpstart on the self-sufficiency that we needed to develop for entrepreneurship.

On Barriers to Success

Entrepreneurial Insight

As an entrepreneur, it may seem as though there are tons of hurdles to overcome. But more than likely you will not overcome any of them without looking risk straight in the eye and moving forward. In a study put out by the Ewing Marion Kauffman Foundation (a Kansas City, Missouri, organization that studies entrepreneurship), 98 percent of those polled said that the biggest barrier to entrepreneurial success was the "lack of willingness or ability to take risks." And there were other barriers, including the time and effort required (93 percent); difficulty raising capital (91 percent); business management skills (89 percent); knowledge about how to start a business (84 percent); industry and market knowledge (83 percent); and family/financial pressures to keep a traditional, steady job (73 percent). Surprising? Not really. No one ever said entrepreneurship was easy. Then again, few things in life that are this satisfying come without difficulty.

Consider the case of Jeff Hoffman, a cofounder of what ultimately became Priceline.com and other Internet companies (as well as executive producer of *Hostel* and *Cabin Fever*, horror films that grossed $180 million and more than $33 million, respectively). Growing up in Phoenix, Arizona, Hoffman saw entrepreneurship figure into his life early on with a paper route in the 1970s. He realized almost immediately that hard work provided sure access to life's good things. "That was a big deal to me, because it granted me independence," he explains. And back in the 1970s, that independence empowered him to buy what he wanted most: baseball cards. The paper route also featured an added bonus of reflection time. Hoffman delivered papers to a lot of big homes, including that of famed director Steven Spielberg, who was already making small films. Riding through those neighborhoods in the quiet dawn, Hoffman passed some time wondering what his clients did for a living in order to afford homes there.

By the time Hoffman reached high school, he had outgrown his paper route; however, he quickly found other ways to produce an income, including selling plant seeds and, later, books. "It wasn't about the money," he notes, "but I liked having money in my pocket for the work I did. I liked that you could go do something you wanted to. I liked the feeling that hard work and freedom could give you, even then." And unlike some of his peers, Hoffman never had to beg his parents for anything. He had the gratifying experience of being able to pay his way with his own earnings.

As it turned out, Hoffman didn't know any other path. "That entrepreneurial mind-set was part of my DNA," he says, adding that his mother produced an income by launching businesses, including a property management venture that served Canadian clients who liked to spend their winters in Arizona. "Her actions are what produced results," Hoffman points out. "She started a company and wrote to these owners. It was a tough row to hoe, as most of her competitors were men. But her example showed me that if there was a will, there was a way." Starting a business might strike fear in some, Hoffman notes, but watching his mother build a successful enterprise showed him that entrepreneurship was possible.

Regrettably, not all of us have entrepreneurial role models to emulate as Hoffman did. In fact, more than half of the entrepreneurs surveyed in a report by the Kauffman Foundation said they were the first in their families to start a business venture. Those of us with role models might not have been as surprised at some of the obstacles we would encounter as these novices were.

When Hoffman graduated from high school, he craved a lot more than baseball cards. Once accepted by Yale University, Hoffman wanted more than anything to enroll there; however, coming up with the tuition proved to be a challenge. And because he was offered scholarships to colleges closer to home, his parents didn't see Yale as a must-attend. So Hoffman enrolled anyway and turned to what he always knew—entrepreneurship—as his ticket, this time into prestigious Yale University. When he was confronted by Yale's treasurer and asked to cough up tuition, "I started my first company my first year at Yale," Hoffman recalls. "I didn't do it because I was smart and wanted experience; it was simply the only option I had: either work or go home."

At this time it was the early 1980s. Software was new, and Hoffman knew he could make money in it. So he began bidding on work for accounting and law firms. There was no stopping him. As Hoffman tells it, "I wrote proposals. I studied hard. I went to companies and said, 'Do you need any software work done?'"

His sales acumen proved to be his greatest strength, and soon Hoffman was amassing clients. There was just one rather substantial flaw: "I didn't know how to create software," he says with a laugh. So he went to local high schools and Yale's computer department and hired people to write the software for him. Hoffman would then mark up the price, and every time he received a check, he'd pay his tuition—and that's how he afforded his Ivy League education. As time went on, Hoffman learned to write the software himself—and at that point, Yale itself became one of his clients. "The school was my biggest customer, ironically," he says. "My favorite project was rewriting the tuition billing system when I was a student."

Entrepreneurial Insight

Some entrepreneurs, who grow up watching their parents try to launch a business, learn early on that when there is a will, almost anything is possible.

Joe Corcoran, the New York producer who helped make *Tony and Tina's Wedding* the second-longest-running show in off-Broadway history, saw the rewards of entrepreneurship early on. "I always knew I'd be in my own business, even as a little kid," says Corcoran. As a former Wall Streeter, Corcoran began to fully realize his entrepreneurial talents during his college years, when he ran mini boat cruises, complete with beer and food, for which he charged $30 a ticket. "I thought it would be fun," says Corcoran, who during his early years had a paper route on Long Island. "I was always doing these kinds of things. Get enough people on a bus for a ski trip, and you go for free. I always had summer jobs, always worked." For Corcoran, entrepreneurship was *fun*—which was a key element to the success behind *Tony and Tina's Wedding*, an interactive performance where the audience gets to party as if they were at a close friend's wedding. His experiences prove that the old mantra is true: If you love what you do, work becomes much easier. In fact, it hardly seems like work at all.

Entrepreneurial Insight

This old mantra is true: If you love what you do, "work" becomes that much easier. In fact, it hardly seems like work at all.

Corcoran grew up in suburbia on the proverbial wrong side of the tracks. Despite its difficulties, the environment in which he spent his youth helped him to establish a strong work ethic. His mother was a homemaker, raising five kids, while his father earned a moderate salary at a big company where Corcoran worked summers. "A lot of my friends came from a lot more money than we did," he says. "I went to parties and people's houses and said, 'Wow, look at this house,' and met the parents. I wasn't intimidated. It was nice to grow up in that environment to see what it could be."

Yet the power of money doesn't necessarily drive all—or even most—entrepreneurs. In fact, many individuals who launch their own enterprises are often from middle-class or upper-lower-class families (though this demographic is more likely to be motivated by wealth), according to the Kauffman Foundation. Consider, for example, Broadway and off-Broadway producer Ken Davenport. As a member of a well-to-do family, Davenport explains that he was surrounded by entrepreneurship while growing up. As the child of divorce, Davenport was influenced by his parents in divergent ways. His father, a learned man, was born and raised in Bombay and settled in the United States to practice cardiology. His stepfather, on the other hand, never graduated from high school, but he owned one of the most successful construction companies in the New England town where the family lived. "My mother married two polar opposites," Davenport says, looking back. "But they both had a work ethic. My father is 80 years old, my stepfather is 73, and they are both still working." Davenport learned firsthand from both men the benefit of hard work. "It was instilled in me to *want* to work and be successful as early as when I was in the Cub Scouts. I wanted to sell prizes for cash in the back of *Boys' Life* magazine."

It's therefore not surprising to learn that Davenport went into business for himself as a kid. "I wanted to get out there and start working and making money," he recalls. "I'm not sure where it came from, unless it was genetic. I wasn't desperate for money, but when I saw my parents working so hard, I wanted to do the same." For that reason, Davenport started to sell candy from his father's cardiology office through an enterprise he called Kenneth's Kandy Shop. His dad taught him about wholesaling—how to buy a box of candy for five dollars and sell individual portions for 50 cents apiece.

Davenport's father's participation in his son's entrepreneurial endeavors is a clear example of how parents constantly send messages to their kids that may unwittingly influence their future. My own mom tried many times to start up businesses when I was a kid; however, she found it impossible to prevail as an entrepreneur while also being a single working parent raising three boys. Still, thanks to her resiliency, we never wanted for anything or did without. My dad, on the other hand, was always the dedicated, hardworking employee. Though neither of them ever sat me down and talked strategy the way Davenport's dad did, I learned a lot from them simply by observing the best aspects of each parent and applying these traits to my own business and professional life. When I launched my own payroll company, I was new to the industry.

But I took my mom's willingness to try new things and added my dad's steadfastness while I was still young and had few responsibilities. I may not have realized it at the time, but these early influences helped me triumph in business.

Entrepreneurial Insight

One of the best traits you can have as an entrepreneur is resiliency.

Davenport continued his entrepreneurial exploration when he began selling knives through a company called Cutco Cutlery while attending college. It was during the recession of the early 1990s, and there was a scarcity of jobs in Massachusetts. But Davenport was somewhat wowed by Cutco's inventory, which was sold one-on-one. There were scissors that cut pennies and other products, sold only through reps—not stores—an approach that he felt leant a certain cachet. Plus, the company taught him and the other reps how to sell their product. Davenport was in business—though the going wasn't easy. "I got rejected so many times, even kicked out of people's homes," he says. "But I did well enough. I earned 15 percent commission. The process was as follows: You bought a sample kit. The more you sold, the more commission you got. You *could* get 50 percent commission, but I decided that approach wasn't for me." Davenport realized he was not going to sell knives forever, so he made a decision to go back to college; however, he admits that he still has a set of the knives.

Though he certainly didn't love every aspect of selling items from candy to knives, Davenport's early lessons served him well. "I was the type of salesman who could absolutely sell the product if I believed in it," he says. It's a skill not unlike raising funds for a Broadway production. If the salesman is truly inspired, his enthusiasm shines through.

For Davenport, passion clearly was a key ingredient for ringing up sales. And while it's essential to believe in the product or service you are selling, the passion for success itself can be the ultimate motivator. I'd be the first to admit that by specializing in payroll, my company hardly provides a very sexy commodity. Yet I am without question passionate about the process of building a business, and that means cultivating relationships and delivering an excellent product and service. When you're passionate about your offering's success, investors take note.

Consider the experience of David Becker, president of 10-year-old San Francisco branding and packaging agency Philippe Becker, whose clients include big brand names such as Starbucks, Safeway, and Whole Foods, to name just a few. Becker likes to clear his head by skydiving. While it's a pursuit that many would label precarious, it's one that he calls "a misunderstood activity." Sure, it involves risk; but Becker minimizes the risk by choosing the proper equipment, receiving the right amount of training, and judging whether or not to go. The approach he takes here is one that helps him a lot in business.

In fact, one might say that Becker's professional life is simply another exercise in balancing risk, since a big part of his work involves convincing clients to consider new concepts and visions for a brand. Becker sees entrepreneurship as "creating something that wasn't previously there"—something for which "you need vision, drive, and a willingness to step into an area where no one's stepped before."

That takes confidence—and, yes, a willingness to take risks. "We're not here to squeak along; we're here to do something big," Becker asserts. "If you want big rewards, you've got to take risks. If you do what's prescribed, you're not going to do anything big."

Entrepreneurial Insight

Enthusiasm coupled with a solid product or service can help an entrepreneur gain entry into almost any marketplace.

It's this bigger reality that is arguably the ultimate risk an entrepreneur can take. Because when you put yourself truly out there—as an artist, professional, or brand—there is literally nowhere to hide. Either your fans and/or customers like you or they don't. This is something I recognized firsthand when launching *Basso On Business*, a web show that I hosted to help fellow entrepreneurs recognize and overcome the challenges they faced in order to grow their businesses.

If the show had been a flop, my reputation would have suffered, since my name is right there on the brand, front and center, and my image is directly on the line. Talk about making myself vulnerable! But perhaps that aspect is what helps propel me forward to produce each new episode and aim to make it better than the last.

Scott Snibbe, CEO of Snibbe Interactive, has built his company's name around the concept of art, community, and technology. His San Francisco firm creates interactive installations for museums, theme parks, theaters, and other locations. Snibbe uses technology to capture the movement of the human body on screens, mirrors, and more to interact through expression. "My whole motivation is trying to build a business making something that's beautiful, meaningful, socially engaging, and enhances people's ability to communicate," Snibbe says. According to him, it's the kind of installation one must experience to fully realize—an innovation that you might not know you were missing if you didn't see it for yourself. It's a business, Snibbe claims, at which he arrived through creativity and innovation. Treading somewhat into no-man's-land takes a certain kind of conviction, a quality to which Snibbe says he was consistently exposed in his childhood.

"My parents were artists," he says. "They worked in technology—which was plastics at the time—and in sculpture as well. My dad made a geometric kite, a perpetual motion machine that creates more energy than it consumes. In essence, it breaks the laws of physics. My dad was also a cabinet maker."

As the children of artists, Snibbe and his brother and sister lived unconventionally. "Growing up, we had no TV; we had a shop where we'd make whatever items we desired, using whatever tools we wanted. My parents wanted us to be creative, to do whatever we wanted with our lives."

For Snibbe, that pursuit was a mix of artist/scientist/inventor, which he carried into his studies at Brown University and eventually to the Rhode Island School of Design. Snibbe then sought out a career vehicle to satisfy these urges. He wasn't naive about the reality of his chosen career; he knew by observing his parents that he'd have difficulty making a living as a full-time artist. However, he wasn't afraid to forge his own path. That was something he learned from his parents as well, who thought nothing of allowing Snibbe and his siblings to stay home from school and create things in the shop. "They taught us that we had to make our own decisions. If you know that something is right for you, you have to travel in that direction. This guidance gave each one of us a real independent streak," says Snibbe, who adds that it did occasionally cause trouble in school for himself and his siblings. But at the same time, Snibbe explains, he was always learning, even on those days when he opted to skip school. "Because my parents were artists, they treated our interests seriously and taught us professional techniques." The guidance that Snibbe's parents provided helped him to build his success as he forged his way through his company into largely unchartered territory.

Sometimes parents can even nurture their children and shape their destiny without necessarily knowing much about the particular industry in which they have an interest. This was the case for Evan Lamberg. Though Lamberg doesn't own a business, he's been downright entrepreneurial in building a successful career in the music field and working with such artists as Rob Thomas of Matchbox Twenty. Today, he serves as Executive Vice President of Creative at Universal Music Publishing Group's East Coast division.

"I had spent three years as a pre-med student at SUNY Albany. I was a year away from applying to medical school and taking my MCATs, and I was a little disgruntled," Lamberg reveals. "Sensing that I wasn't happy with the path I'd chosen, my mother suggested that I might be better suited for the music industry. She even went so far as to do some research at the library, and found a program at NYU for music and business." For Lamberg—who used to stay up late reading *Billboard* magazine as a 13-year-old in order to catch up on music producers and labels—the program offered him the chance to enter an industry where he had no connections. All he had were parents who went the extra mile, simply because his mother wanted to see him happy and spending his time doing something he loved. Lamberg explains gratefully that this switch from medicine to music "shaped my entire life."

Perhaps the key ingredient needed to break through as a talented artist is a role model who focuses and perseveres. Take, for example, fashion designer and *Project Runway* contestant Ari Fish. "I had my first job when I was thirteen. I worked illegally (because of my age) at a Best Western as a maid. My mother worked as a night auditor there, as well as both a substitute teacher and a college professor."

Fish saw her mother build what she called an empire. Was it an empire, truly? That hardly matters, as the definition of such a claim is truly in the eye of the beholder. But whether it was attaining unprecedented wealth or supporting her family on her own terms, Fish saw her mother call her own shots, something that served for her as the ultimate inspiration. As Fish puts it, "I wanted to do the same, in my own way."

Fish had a penchant for independence and a complete absence of fear, mixed with a quest to keep moving forward. As she explains, "I believe the most innovative designers are those who are at first self-taught—those who had such a dire need to design that they gave it a go with all the naïveté of a child and the ambition of a warrior. We are trained from the beginning to be self-sufficient if we want anything done right—and by 'right' I mean designed and produced to some otherworldly bizarre standard."

Entrepreneurial Insight

Perhaps the best formula for innovation is creativity, with a healthy dose of conviction.

Not all successful businesspersons had parents who taught them to take risks. Nor do they always have entrepreneurs in their families. Entrepreneurial DNA is probably not enough to triumph. There's a lot more than this at play, all of which we examine in the next chapters.

Everyday Case Study/Less Stress for Success

Subject Business: Ultimate Class Limousine and Ground Transportation

Owner Name: Matt Silver

View Video at: www.BassoOnBusiness.com

Ultimate Class is run by a brash leader named Matt Silver, who is ever-present on the regional networking and charity circuit.

In fact, I would say that he knows more people in the New York/ New Jersey/Connecticut area than any other human being. Silver runs a fleet of cars, buses, vans, and limos that deliver prom-goers, professionals, and soon-to-be-married couples to and from their destinations within a reasonable price point and with professional service. Sounds great, right?

The only problem is that Matt has spent many years working so feverishly to ensure his clients were well taken care of that he has neglected his own peace of mind. In fact, Matt's stress level was at an all-time high when the Basso On Business team visited his location. Matt answers the phone, jumps in a car himself if a driver does not show up, and even takes reservations. When we arrived at the Ultimate Class facility, we were immediately impressed by the number of vehicles in his garage. We were further astounded by the very small number of staff members working in the office to make his business machine hum. Then we sat back and observed.

Matt was a virtual whirlwind. He would do anything and everything that needed to be completed the minute the task came up on his radar. And while he performed enviably and without a misstep, he did so at a price. Matt confided in us that after more than 20 years running his company, he felt that the stress was beginning to take its toll. He realized he needed to find a way to manage his business more efficiently and take steps to reduce his stress level to ensure he kept himself healthy enough to enjoy his family and the fruits of his success.

To prove the point that he was a bit overwhelmed, we saved a voice message he left on my business phone. He was confirming the appointment for my team to come down and tape our show at his office. The only problem was that he was calling a week early, a half hour late—and headed in the wrong location. He was clearly overloaded and needed to make some changes.

Matt was using an outdated handwritten agenda book for all the appointments he needed to keep. He did carry a Black-Berry for e-mail purposes, but for some reason did not use that

(continued)

(*continued*)

technology to keep his appointments straight. We asked him what would happen if he lost his agenda book, and we received a blank stare in return. It was clear that he would be utterly lost without this item, and this would certainly cause even greater stress.

Matt also had an incredibly exhausting networking schedule that often kept him out six nights a week. It was becoming very burdensome, since every night he was out meant another night that he wasn't home with his family after working long hours all day. There is only so much of that anyone's family and business can take. The economy was tough; because Matt had seen several smaller local companies fail, he felt it necessary to put in the extra networking hours in order to keep his business afloat.

We worked through some simple suggestions that Matt has since implemented in his business; these have helped reduce his stress levels and have created a more efficient operation. First, we got Matt up to speed on using the BlackBerry for all his appointments. It's not that there was anything wrong with his paper agenda; it was just that he didn't have any backup if he lost it. Using the BlackBerry presented a more practical solution, since he carried the unit anyway to use as a phone and e-mail source.

Matt realized he could not jump on the phone every time it rang; instead, he needed to spend his time bringing in new business. To fill this gap in his office, he hired a part time reservationist to fill some open time in his staffing. This has helped dramatically in raising productivity and reducing stress. As for Matt jumping in cars if a driver is out, I would hazard a guess he still does it occasionally; however, he told me that it doesn't happen nearly as much as it used to. He also implemented some infrastructure changes to make sure that there is always someone available for backup if a staff member can't make a pick-up.

Perhaps most importantly, Matt reduced his networking schedule significantly, and is now more selective about where and when to go to make sure he maximizes his opportunities. As for adding help in the sales department, it appears Matt thrives on this aspect of his job and enjoys being the rainmaker.

That's perfectly fine as long as he realizes that his overall growth could be limited while he is the only one prospecting for new business.

SUMMARY

- Get organized and use technology to stay on top of your tasks and appointments.
- Delegate properly to ensure tasks are handled appropriately and empower your staff to do it.
- Pick your battles in the marketplace. You can't be everywhere all the time, so be selective in the events you attend.
- Realize that reducing stress will increase productivity.

Information taken from a personal interview with Matt Silver on June 4, 2010; video © Basso On Business, Inc.

Summary

Entrepreneurs, by their very nature, are a motivated lot. They are not afraid to blaze their own trail to success, creating a path of independence along the way. In addition, many of them:

- Learned to be self-reliant as kids, whether they did so by holding part-time jobs such as paper routes, or watching their parents try to create their own ventures.
- Are resourceful and able to figure out a way around barriers to entry.
- Find entrepreneurship fun, even when facing tough challenges.
- Thrive on the successes they have, which helps them to persevere.
- Bring a level of enthusiasm to the table that helps open doors and bring in orders.
- Are passionate about doing something *big*.
- Add creativity to the mix, whether it's charting a new direction or producing something new in the market.
- Are sometimes lucky enough to have a role model or mentor who makes risk-taking much easier.

2

Take the Blinders Off

WHEN YOU ARE young and inexperienced in business, you run into snags—a lot of snags. But as nice as it might seem to be able to predict all the challenges you'll face, there is an upside to not seeing those lurking hurdles. Having this sort of no-worries-in-sight belief system lends a certain freedom to the way you pursue opportunities. This is especially true when you're entering new terrain, such as introducing something that the market has not necessarily seen before. Uninhibited resourcefulness can determine the difference between making it in business or not. (Then again, if you knew your actions might trigger unfavorable consequences, maybe you never would have pursued the opportunity in the first place!)

As Broadway producer Ken Davenport puts it, "I don't know the definition of the term 'boundary.' So I just go forward and don't allow anything to get in the way. The moment I label something as 'difficult,' I slow down. And that prevents me from moving forward."

Davenport's point is clear: Unlike most other individuals, entrepreneurs like to push forward. "They are like freight trains that can barrel through," Davenport says. "If you are an engineer who sees a snow bank, you'll slow down." However, it stands to reason that an entrepreneur will find a way around the snow bank, or simply storm through it.

Talk to forthcoming entrepreneurs who have spent time in the trenches, and more than likely they will regale you with stories of their naïveté and consequential setbacks. However, many will also share their comebacks, their tales of conquering obstacles, and the lessons they learned as they picked themselves up and kept going. A common quality that these entrepreneurs share is that they are inclined to push past hurdles and are never satisfied with "no." That is not to say that successful entrepreneurs tend to be obstinate or refuse to see how things truly are. But they do know—and always will—how come up with a plan B, and a C and a D if needed. And this is a good thing. Indeed, it is the surest way to get that all-important support from contacts, employees, vendors, and contractors. Without that buy-in, many of us would never make it past week two.

It's no secret that in order to flourish in business, you need favors. Maybe you need a creditor to extend payment another 30 days, or to get a prospect to consider an alternative solution in order to salvage a deal. That kind of support does not happen by itself. It's a simple but undeniable fact: People like doing business with the people they like. So somehow these entrepreneurs strike an interesting balance: They appeal to others without compromising their integrity, as they are on constant guard and always looking for a way to remain viable. Are they pushy? Sometimes, yes. But behind that pushiness is a profoundly deep commitment to their mission. That steadfastness triggers good things.

Entrepreneurial Insight

Entrepreneurs, as a rule, never shrink back, no matter how high the stakes.

They seem to know intrinsically that there is very little opportunity to coast. Very few of us have the luxury of establishing ourselves at the beginning of our careers and enjoying a single, incredibly successful ride (though it might look that way). If you believe that you only need to set yourself up once and never have to reconfigure, restrategize, or even bail out, then you risk losing everything.

Naïveté Can Actually Help You Get Started

When you're young, ambitious, and hungry for success, you'll stop at nothing to gain momentum, seizing opportunities that the more seasoned deem unworthy or even foolish. But Joe Corcoran held so much conviction for the fun to be had at the show *Tony and Tina's Wedding* that he put his heart and soul into making it work.

"It was my first show," Corcoran says. "Had I had more experience, I may have passed. It has 27 actors, an audience of 150, and requires us to serve a meal. There was not a high gross potential. It had two venues: a church, and then everyone went down the block to eat. My naïveté caused me to believe in the show so much that

I pursued it. If I had known then what I know today, I might be a bit more jaded—which could have prevented me from following my passion."

Corcoran and his brother had plowed ahead with showcases in 1985 and again in 1987. The second show intrigued *People* magazine, which wound up doing a four-page spread on it, coverage that "made the show immediately legitimate," Corcoran says. He adds that it has since been featured in hundreds of publications and television shows, where cameras highlighted people laughing and dancing, helping to draw in new audiences.

Corcoran followed an important rule in business success: He perceived a demand, and he hung in there for as long as the venture proved viable. However, he also understood that this viability is open to interpretation and that there is no single magic formula. There is a fine line between keeping an effort going and knowing when to quit. More seasoned producers may have walked away sooner than Corcoran; but then again, they would never have achieved the wild success Corcoran eventually realized with *Tony and Tina's Wedding*. He saw the demand for the entertainment that his show fulfilled, and he was able to hang in there until the press ultimately validated that demand and prompted the public to catch wind of the show's fun. By then, the buzz was contagious.

Entrepreneurial Insight

Perceive a demand, and hang in there for as long as the venture proves viable. But that viability is open to interpretation—there is no single magic formula.

No Room for Weak Links

In a world where survival is for the fittest, the weak either need to build up their character or step aside. It's kind of like boxing, an activity with which I have firsthand experience. I can attest to the fact that if you train, you can build up the endurance to withstand almost anything—something that's incredibly reassuring when you find yourself in the ring, struggling to make it through the next round and ultimately win. Business is a lot like this. If you enter a market prepared, knowing everything possible about its demographics and the products and services that could work there, you can make it to the next round and become a decision maker. But it's a matter of having the right tools, especially the ability to apply logic.

Priceline cofounder Jeff Hoffman learned this lesson early on. For Hoffman, shrinking back just never seemed to make sense, even as a kid. Why would it, when he was rewarded enough times for pushing past obstacles?

"I have always been one to wonder why and question everything," Hoffman says. It is an ability that served him in business, but also in high school, when—like most students—Hoffman felt he had better things to do than homework. But the difference between him and his peers was that Hoffman was actually able to convince his teacher of the same. As Hoffman explained, he owed his Spanish teacher three days' worth of homework because he played on the school's football team, and finishing assignments just were not a priority. And Hoffman saw no reason not to question authority. His conversation with the Spanish teacher went something like this:

Teacher: Homework is not optional.
Hoffman: Why do you even give us homework?
Teacher: So you can learn.
Hoffman: How do you know what I've learned? How about if I ace the test I don't have to do the homework?

To Hoffman's surprise, the teacher agreed. When students found out about it and complained, the teacher offered them the same deal—ace the test and they, too, could skip the homework.

Entrepreneurial Insight

When questioning the rules, suggest a reasonable alternative on which all of the stakeholders can agree.

Hoffman never accepted rules, and instead asked people to explain them. Then he would hit them up with his logic and offer an alternative. When it really counted, Hoffman succeeded in convincing others to buy into his reasoning. It's a formula that works in the business world as well.

Entrepreneurial Insight

Push boundaries, but keep your integrity intact.

You cannot be shy about pushing limits. Some may hesitate to test boundaries, but in business, there are no inappropriate questions when the end result could ultimately add value to a process, whether it helps to save time or money.

Watch Those Toes

Personally, I was never much for working for someone else. So when I was looking to make some quick cash over the summer while in college, I bought a couple of ice cream truck routes and hired some friends as drivers. However, I soon realized that no one hands you a rulebook that breaks down protocols when you go into business. Even if such a book did exist, it's fairly obvious that many entrepreneurs don't take rules sitting down. When you don't know the boundaries of expected practices, there is nothing to hold you back. Then again, without boundaries, you might step in some pretty murky water.

That was the case with my ice cream truck business. Surprisingly, the routes were profitable, and my drivers were entrepreneurial in maximizing sales by knowing which streets generated the most customers at what time. But little did they know they were actually encroaching on someone else's territory. Suddenly, they—and by default, I—were immersed in an ice cream turf war where we looked like poachers. I didn't want it to get ugly, but I also didn't want to hurt my own bottom line. So, like an athlete looking to the ref when there's a foul, I turned to the company that leased me the trucks to come up with a resolution by which we could all abide. We held a meeting with the other driver on whose territory we had encroached, and we came to an understanding about the proper protocol to follow. We agreed to stick to our routes, and we did our best to maximize our revenues. I had to think quickly in order to keep profits up. After all, with such a short season, time was not on my side, and now that my territory was smaller than I originally believed, I would have fewer opportunities to build profit (I still had to pay my drivers and buy inventory). In a flash, I adapted a "Want fries with that?" mentality. I made up for the loss in territory by up-selling products. We had priced ice cream cones at $1.50 and knew that our customers, mostly kids, had two quarters left. We simply started asking the question, "Would you like a lollipop for later? They are only 25 cents." The lollipop would not melt, the kids had a sweet treat for later on, and we increased sales. It was a lesson in pushing the boundaries as far as possible without compromising our own integrity.

Entrepreneurial Insight

As a business owner, you may work for yourself. But that does not mean you don't have to play nicely with others. Far from it. You need employees, investors, vendors, customers, and prospects to be on your side. So, try to work with the other personalities, no matter how difficult they may sometimes be. Remember: This is in the best interest of your business.

However, turf wars don't merely begin and end on the ice cream beat. Years later, after I had built Advantage Payroll into a money-making enterprise, I launched a new, complementary venture. At this point I was age 30—young, but no kid. Yet I was dabbling in a new kind of territory, one that hadn't really been explored before, at least not in my region.

I knew my industry inside and out, and I was already serving as a valuable resource to clients and prospects who were looking for related business services; some needed benefits and insurance providers, others needed credit card processing providers. I had access to them all. And most importantly, I had solid business relationships with everyone, from clients to vendors and everyone in between. So I founded a firm called Cossential that matched companies seeking services with prequalified vendors at a better price than they could get independently. I threw a fantastic launch party at Republic Airport, a local airport for small and corporate planes that was outside the usual meeting spots. I had selected the venue carefully to show my audience that this offering was no ordinary venture—that I valued them so much, I wanted to treat them to a memorable evening out. There was plenty of goodwill all around.

Or so I thought.

I soon discovered, however, that I had again unintentionally stepped on people's turf by wandering into territories that others had already claimed as their own. I was inadvertently pitting vendors against vendors, and sometimes even competing with my own payroll clients as we both vied for the same audience. Also, not everyone got the value of the service. In the end, Cossential caused more headaches than it was worth. It was a disappointment, and yet another turf war lesson learned. You would think that the ice cream truck challenge would have helped me get this right, but I suppose that reinforcement is needed sometimes. They do not teach this stuff in business school—and I won't make this mistake again.

Entrepreneurial Insight

Keep territories in mind. You do not want to erode your own base.

Even through Cossential never really took off, I would hardly call the pursuit a loss. I've since closed the company and started providing some of these value-added services through the Advantage brand. There is a definite market for these vendor-approved services, and it helps that I learned to package them differently and not step on too many toes. While I'm certainly not against ruffling a few feathers, it helps to learn which ones to ruffle, and when it's best to do so.

Entrepreneurial Insight

Start thinking about your plan B, even if you think you won't need it. This is a good exercise in becoming resourceful.

Everyday Case Study/Stop Planning and Get Selling

Subject Business: Sandwire, Inc.

Owner Name: Adam Schwam

View Video at: www.BassoOnBusiness.com

Sandwire is an IT infrastructure and back-up solutions provider for hundreds of businesses in the New York metropolitan area. Owner Adam Schwam is extremely bright and motivated, despite the fact the he never completed high school. He does have his GED and Schwam has not allowed the absence of a high school diploma to keep him from building a formidable company.

I first met Adam nearly 10 years ago when we were both involved in starting a nonprofit business group called The Long Island Elite, which facilitates opportunities for its members and donates all profits to local charities. Along the way, Adam and I developed a strong friendship based on mutual respect, often sharing our respective business challenges with each other.

Though Adam provided a quality product, he struggled to market his services in a bigger way, mostly as a result of being mired down in the day-to-day struggles of operating of a business. He was constantly planning projects and initiatives to bring in more revenue, but never actually got around to implementing them. For example, he rented space in a beautiful office building in the heart of an exclusive area at a very high cost, where he had an entire office designated for the sales team he planned to hire. However, when the Basso On

Business crew arrived to shoot Adam's episode, that room was serving as a storage facility—devoid of any salespeople or even sales equipment.

We asked Adam why this was the case. He responded by telling us that he needed to both establish his sales and marketing plan and make sure his CRM tools were in place in order to implement his complete sales system before hiring anyone. While this might seem like a smart idea on the surface, that's not the case if the plan takes two years to complete. Adam struggled with an issue that many entrepreneurs face: using planning as an excuse to simply procrastinate to the point where they never complete or realize projects or objectives.

In Adam's defense, why *wouldn't* he spend his time planning? After all, his analytical mind is very good at putting the pieces together and making sure they fit perfectly so that nothing goes wrong. However, what went wrong in this case was the fact that he lost opportunities along the way while he was planning and not selling. Adam is not oblivious to this fact; he stated that he previously only concentrated on sales in his free time. But you cannot wait to work on sales—the element that drives your company's growth—in your free time if you want your business to achieve exponential growth.

Adam possesses two unique qualities that many in his field do not: He is very conversational, and he is a borderline genius when it comes to implementing systems and networks. While this is a special combination for sure, he needed to get out of his own way to stop planning and start selling. The timing would never be absolutely right, and the launch would never be perfect, but he had to move forward—even incrementally, if possible. Small business owners don't have the extensive budget for research and analysis that larger organizations do, so we have to learn along the way. Otherwise, none of our planning or initiatives will ever come to fruition.

Since we visited, Adam has decided to move out of his expensive space to a more appropriate location. He realized

(continued)

(*continued*)

that, due to his business's back-office nature, he does did not need to be in a high-profile, high-rent district. He also has spent a significantly greater amount of time actually *selling* his services. While he did not go out and hire a sales team as he initially intended, he did plot a course to pass off administrative work to his staff so he could focus on bringing in new accounts himself. His business is growing and he's picking up more clients on a more consistent basis, because he got back to the basics of employing simple time management tools and goal-setting techniques. Adam used to spend hours on the proposal process even for smaller jobs; however, he's now systematized this procedure so that it takes only a fraction of the time. As a direct result, he can spend more time in front of potential clients and better lead his company.

The time we shared with Adam was well spent, and he has made significant progress since we were there. In fact, there was an unintended but nonetheless important result from the time we shared with him that we could have never imagined. After seeing himself on camera, Adam was appalled at how unhealthy and overweight he looked. Adam has since lost more than 40 pounds and has taken a more healthy approach to his overall lifestyle. We never imagined that we would be able to help him with his business and his physical health all in the same show.

Adam and Sandwire share the same challenges that most small businesses face. Learning from his own mistakes will ensure Adam's continued growth and success.

SUMMARY

- Beware of the tendency to overplan; this can kill your business's growth.
- Keep your overhead low and select appropriate facilities.
- The timing will never be perfect; you just have to start somewhere.
- You're completely allowed to change or break plans if it helps you meet your end results.

- It is important to have goals, but only if you actually plan on trying to achieve them.
- Use your strengths to help your business thrive.
- Your physical health is just as important to the success of your business as your balance sheet.

Information taken from a personal interview with Adam Schwam on March 10, 2010; video © Basso On Business, Inc.

Assessing, Reassessing, and Constantly Learning

I walked away from my experience with Cossential a better businessperson, even though I did not achieve the results I thought were possible. It's all a matter of looking at the data you have, and making your best judgment in determining how to reposition yourself, which components are worth salvaging, or whether to simply call it a day.

For Selena Cuffe, however, folding was simply not an option. In 2005, Cuffe founded Heritage Link Brands, a Los Angeles–based importer of wines produced by indigenous Africans and those of African descent. Despite having everything mapped out perfectly—or so she thought—Cuffe was forced to resort to a plan B that she had to configure on the fly.

As a Harvard Business School graduate who had worked on launches for big name brands like Tampax and Pringles, Cuffe walked away from a lucrative job to start Heritage Link Brands. Cuffe describes the market this way: "Nobody has that equity in the diaspora, and that enabled us to attract a lot of curiosity; it's what made us different." So naturally, Cuffe was excited to get the green light from grocery chain Whole Foods, through which her company was planning to launch their product.

However, Cuffe almost didn't make it out of the gate. At the final hour, the rep who was supposed to deliver the product went AWOL. Here they were, about to meet the Whole Foods buyer, and they had nothing to offer. If she wanted to remain credible to this important client, Cuffe had to think fast under very dicey circumstances.

"We were going to shut down," Cuffe concedes. "We went to Whole Foods and said, 'There was a product supply issue. Would you consider a new product?'"

As it turned out, the answer was yes, and to favorable results. "The new product worked out even better," Cuffe says. "We learned to diversify and make sure suppliers have the capacity to deliver."

Looking back, Cuffe says, "I thought, 'No is not a possibility. I can't quit.'"

And while any dedicated entrepreneur would have a hard time letting go of a business built from the bootstraps, this was especially true for Cuffe. She had a close-to-the-heart mission to bring fair business practices, civic leadership, and aid to social causes that improve conditions in Africa and its diaspora.

It is easy to see that sometimes business can get personal. Admitting failure and letting down stakeholders is difficult. But knowing when to call it quits can make letting go easier and, if you are savvy enough, sometimes you'll end up with some cash in your pocket to show for all that you put into a venture.

Timing Can Be Everything

Cuffe's experience shows us that, occasionally, obstacles seem to come out of nowhere. And sometimes even when you see the market and the need, your timing could be way off, even if you are an industry leader.

Consider Jeff Hoffman's scenario. Before Internet shopping became a regular pastime, Hoffman had developed a software application for online shopping, and major retailers wanted in. But there was one problem: At the time, "consumers were not ready to shop online," Hoffman explains. "We overestimated. We were just wrong."

There seemed to be two alternatives at that point. As Hoffman puts it, "You either fold up your chair and go home, or you keep going anyway because pride won't let you admit you were wrong. But that second decision can be fatal."

However, Hoffman came up with another plan. He explains: "I was willing to accept that we were wrong, but I wanted to reexamine what we had. We were on this path that led to a dead end, but I said,

'Let's back up, put our assets on the table, stare at them, and ask: Is there something different we can do?'" As it turned out, Hoffman's company had developed the kind of technology in which banks saw an application, and Hoffman was ultimately able to sell the assets.

> ### Entrepreneurial Insight
>
> Even when you think it is time to fold, take one last look at your assets, since you may still have something of value that the market might want.

Sometimes you need a visual to push a new idea along. That is especially true on Broadway, where a showcase can mean the difference between attracting investors or not. Just ask Ken Davenport, who produced the show *Altar Boyz*. Davenport would be the first to point out that a producer looking for investors is not unlike the process of investing in stock. There are ups and downs, and your investors are along for the ride. In fact, Davenport's investors have told him as much by saying, "I'm putting my money in you. If this show doesn't make it, there will be one in the future that does." Of course, it helps to have a hit or two, as Davenport has had with *Altar Boyz* and others. With an off-Broadway debut in 2004, the show went on to win the 2005 Outer Critics Circle Award for Outstanding Off-Broadway Musical.

But Davenport needed to spread his enthusiasm for the show while it was still in its conceptual phase. When he was informed that he needed to raise $1 million, Davenport was undaunted. "I said okay, if that's the amount needed, I'm going to raise it."

> ### Entrepreneurial Insight
>
> Entrepreneurs see hurdles as doable.

While the thought of raising large sums of money puts off many business owners, those like Davenport who believe in their end goal have a good shot at rallying investors to the cause. Davenport, who had worked his way up the ranks in the theater, began by inviting people to readings and rehearsals with actors. He then had his cast and crew put on the show in a musical theater festival, which cost him nearly $40,000. "That festival [allowed me to] raise that million. I don't remember calling people and saying, 'Do you want to put money into this show?' People came to me and said, 'I saw the show. How can I get involved?' When a venture like this works, it works to such an incredible amount people are desperate to get in. When they see an opportunity, they jump all over it, because they know the exponential growth can be incredible."

Still, not every producer can knock it out of the park, not even a successful one like Davenport, who's seen his share of struggles. "One of the biggest challenges is that it's very lonely," says Davenport, who doesn't have a business partner. In particular, Davenport struggled with his first show, *The Awesome 80s Prom*. Behind the scenes, Davenport, who'd written the script, was running a one-man business operation, raising the money, answering the group sales line, handling the box office, and directing. "We had no staff. I was working out of my apartment. My biggest clients were sweet-16 parties. I would get out of bed at 8:30 AM in my boxers and jump desperately to answer the phone. I learned so much about sales. I'd tell parents, 'Yes, we'll take care of your daughters.'"

The ups and downs of launching a show were fast and furious. "There was so much joy to see the audience, but I was losing so much money. I was down to my last $2,000. I was literally in tears." Not quite knowing how to pull through, Davenport feared he would soon be out of money and forced to close the show. But he pulled himself off the floor and decided to trust his instincts and keep going. It was a good thing he did. As luck would have it, things began to turn around the very next day, and the show is still running.

Still, even Davenport knows that there are times when it's best to call it a day. As an example, Davenport points to coming-of-age musical *13*. "I knew the show was a good one, but I also knew, thanks to my financial training, that I had to pull myself out," he says. "I looked at the numbers and realized right away that it wasn't working. That's the hard part—separating emotion from logic. We take part in these projects because we love them like our children; if we are forced to abandon them, we feel like we failed. I could have invested 80 hours of my time to keep this show going, but I had to think about the best way to spend my time. I was thinking about moving it to a new venue because the theater was giving us pressure, but it wasn't worth it, moneywise. I figured I'd gain much more by moving on and doing something else."

However, that doesn't mean Davenport is saying goodbye to the show forever. It could have another life somewhere else—maybe on the road, or at another time. When I shuttered Cossential, I eventually took some concepts from that failure and incorporated them with my core business at Advantage Payroll and had great success with them. Intuitive entrepreneurs, like Davenport, find a way to use bits and pieces of their mistakes and give them a second chance when it is appropriate. I have a distinct feeling that we will see *13* reincarnated sometime in the future.

Entrepreneurs often succeed because they do not see (or heed) the boundaries that tend to hold others back. They manage to rally supporters, largely because people like to back winners. By going the distance, these entrepreneurs cultivate not only a following but also stellar reputations. They also realize how important to it is protect that reputation going forward, a topic we'll look at in Chapter 3.

Entrepreneurial Insight

Rally your supporters. They like to back winners.

Summary

In business, as with any other endeavor, the hurdles can seem to just keep coming. But the more often you're able to leap over them, the more proficient you will become at seeing things from new angles and remaining resourceful. When honing your entrepreneurial chops, keep the following in mind:

- Push past the "no," even if this means coming up with alternate plans in order to stay on track.
- Hold steady, even when the stakes are high.

- Hang in there as long as the venture is viable. But be sure to understand your threshold, and remember that everyone's is different.
- Always apply logic when appealing to the people who can make a difference in your quest.
- Think twice about crossing boundaries and stepping on toes; both of these can backfire.
- Never let ego get in the way, and recognize when it is time to fold.
- Take the time to reevaluate your circumstances. Even if your venture fails, it may still have assets that prove valuable to the market.
- Realize that your investors are putting their money in *you*, not just your business. Give them something to believe in.
- Once you are sure of your proposal and your market, speak about them with confidence.
- Remember that while struggles can be brutal, they are also ripe with learning opportunities that you will likely never forget.
- Never give up completely; a failed venture could have another life sometime in the future.

3

Image and Reputation Matter

THANKS TO THE electronic age in which professionals and companies currently find themselves, reputation and image matter now more than ever before. In this time of seemingly endless social media interaction—where Facebook musings can spread virally like wildfire and Twitter followers can increase by hundreds in mere seconds—anyone can be lifted onto a virtual pedestal when fans sing their praises. However, keep in mind that you can be taken down just as quickly.

As scary as that sounds, this concept is really nothing new to entrepreneurs who put their heart and soul into starting a business, winning over people's trust, and reaching new heights. These entrepreneurs already know instinctively that their reputation is their most valuable asset, and they've been meticulous in not only taking care of how they project their image but also how they maintain it. They know that it is a given when you grow a business that your stakeholders must have complete confidence in you. Otherwise, they will not give you their business, work for you, or go to bat for you. And they will most certainly not introduce you to people of influence.

So this begs the question: When you are just getting started in business, how do you win people's confidence to open the door just enough to give you a shot at proving what you already know—that you can do the job, and do it well? Arguably, the answer is in those first, second, and third impressions, and even beyond them. Maybe you have the expertise required; maybe you don't. But you'd better be able to communicate that you have the ingenuity to live up to your promise. This is the concept that entrepreneurs express, often subliminally. They know how vital it is to convey a favorable image, then over-deliver with outstanding service and products, and then develop a following—a fan base of people who will sing your praises and help you establish a record of accomplishment and integrity.

It's easy for some people to project that kind of image right from the beginning. It helps, of course, if you have the credentials. Take, for example, Selena Cuffe, the CEO of Heritage Link Brands, which imports wines from South Africa. Cuffe received her MBA from

41

Harvard Business School—an icon of the utmost competency, legitimacy, and character. An MBA from Harvard may well be the ultimate door opener for anyone building a business, yet Cuffe continues to work diligently at staying on top of her game. As she puts it, "Before a meeting, I make sure I study up on a particular wine variety—left, right, backwards, and forwards."

Still, Harvard credentials or not, sometimes even the most intense preparation may prove to be not enough. But that doesn't seem to fluster Cuffe. "I never faked my knowledge of my wine," she says. "I'd defer to the winemaker or producer. I try to keep it real." Whenever she was pressed for answers that she could not produce on her own, she would look to an expert who possessed a better understanding than she did.

Most entrepreneurs—myself included—lack that coveted Harvard MBA. Yet, like Cuffe, we have the resourcefulness and determination to keep it real. As it turns out, some of us prove to be just a bit more resourceful than others, all in the name of getting started.

> **Entrepreneurial Insight**
>
> Prepare for the skepticism of prospects, and stay focused on convincing them to take a chance on you.

The Need-to-Know Basis

People may envy youth, but it's no easy task being a 20-something who's attempting to launch his own business. In fact, it's pretty daunting. When I was first starting out, I would arrive at scheduled appointments dressed in my best suit and tie from the low-cost men's clothing store, Today's Man. I showed up looking professional, albeit on a budget. Still, the moment I met the prospect, I recognized that certain look. It was as if I could hear the person speak out loud, wondering if this kid knew what the hell he was doing. It was up to me to prove that I most definitely was 100 percent on top of my game. And I *was* ready. I was prepared for their skepticism and primed to convince them to take a chance on me. I'd researched the company, its people, and if possible, their vendors; I wanted to reveal that not only did I know my stuff but that I cared about *their* success.

However, there were also several things I was careful not to do. For instance, unless they asked, I never let on that I actually owned the company I was representing. It was difficult enough to take me seriously as a capable sales rep, let alone a serious entrepreneur. I also never parked my old Nissan Sentra where it would be visible from the client's entrance, opting instead for a nearby lot. My business rented what amounted to a storage room in the basement of a building with a decent address on Long Island, and I always met potential clients on their territory, not mine. After all, image matters; don't let anyone tell you otherwise.

Entrepreneurial Insight

Craft your image, but keep it real. Your reputation matters.

To help build the image I wanted to present as a leading, energetic professional, I hired a public relations firm to put me top of mind with business leaders in the region. Soon, I was quoted in some of the area's most-read publications. People were beginning to know my name and recognize me as someone with a solid reputation.

It's Okay to Embellish—But Just a Little

> *If you said the truth exactly where things were, you'd never get out of the starting gate.*
> —Steve Davies, founder, US Computer Group

Some entrepreneurs may find it advantageous to help an image along if it tells the kind of story prospects feel is important. Just a caveat, though: This scenario can work in your favor only when you can absolutely deliver on customer satisfaction, as Steve Davies will tell you.

Davies is a seasoned entrepreneur with a degree from Oxford University who had a successful career at Barclays Bank in England before relocating to New York and launching US Computer Group. The organization placed on the *Inc.* 500 list of fastest-growing companies, and it was even inducted into the *Inc.* Hall of Fame. Yet his firm—like so many others—was virtually unknown before it achieved such recognition, and Davies had to rely on his wits to get clients to believe in his ability to deliver.

"When I started my computer service company, people wanted to make sure that I had the spare parts to take on the contract," Davies recalls. Davies had an arrangement with another company to get these parts as needed, but that agreement was not something he necessarily wanted to broadcast. "I knew we could do the work, but we didn't have spares on site. So when we were close to getting a contract, we put some empty boxes on the shelves. I never said we had the parts, so I never viewed this as being deceitful. If everyone told the truth exactly as it is, no one would ever get out of the starting gate."

Those boxes served as a visual that told a story and made a promise Davies knew he could keep. It was not a technique that Davies used often. But he was confident that he would do whatever it took to win the job and not only meet but exceed customer expectations. Could it have backfired? Sure. But Davies took that risk, with determination to succeed on his side.

"I knew I could deliver," Davies says. "It's like a swan swimming with its feet going like hell beneath the surface. We had a strong ethic delivering what we said. We never compromised the service. That enabled us to grow and get more work. We grew 45 percent a year for eight consecutive years. In 10 years, we went from nothing to a $25-million-a-year company." Like the swan that looked calm on the surface, US Computer Group put on a composed public face; however, they were working as hard as they could behind the scenes to fill the orders that were rapidly coming in.

While storytelling helped Davies build his business, he stayed clear of embellishing his core competencies. With his resources lined up, he knew he could always deliver—and that is critical in cultivating your name.

> ### Entrepreneurial Insight
>
> When investors have confidence in you, they may actively seek you out to see how they can back one of your new projects.

Waking Up Any Sleeping Dogs

In the social media age, word spreads virally and rapidly. Sites such as Twitter, Facebook, and Yelp, among others, allow clients, employees, vendors, and others to compliment your services and put you on a virtual pedestal for the entire world to see. Yet a dissatisfied customer, associate, or partner can also take to the Internet and condemn you just as loudly.

> ### Entrepreneurial Insight
>
> While social media might have begun as a pastime for the young, a growing number of older people rely on these platforms to stay in touch, not just with family and friends but also with colleagues, companies, and customers, according to the Pew Internet & American Life Project. What's more, this group found that people are now "especially attuned to the intricacies of online reputation management," whether they are looking to market themselves or to fly beneath the radar.

For this reason, it is critical to address all online criticisms in real time. This was exemplified when mobile telephone operator Vodafone launched a campaign called The 12 Days of Smiles, in which Twitter users were supposed to tweet about something that made them happy. But angry protesters launched an assault on the company during the campaign, claiming that Vodafone had neglected to pay its fair share of taxes in the United Kingdom. The company not only failed to remove the postings, they also failed to respond to the slew of angry tweets. Vodafone missed an opportunity to have a genuine conversation and set the record straight.

It does not matter whether you are a large public company or a small business owner in Idaho; the negative repercussions of such a public blunder can leave a lasting mark on any organization's reputation.

Entrepreneurial Insight

In the age of social media, word spreads fast, perhaps landing you and your company in the limelight—whether you want to be there or not.

At the same time, however, entrepreneurs can put social media to work *for* them, by creating a base of loyal fans who are eager to hear your thoughts. That was the case for New Jersey wine retailer Gary Vaynerchuk, who produced an online show called *Wine Library TV*. According to the *New York Times*, Vaynerchuk ultimately garnered an estimated 90,000 viewers and close to 900,000 Twitter followers, all of whom were eager to hear him opine about various wines. The effort landed him in the spotlight with book publishing deals as well as television appearances on both *The Ellen DeGeneres Show* and *Late Night with Conan O'Brien*. However, Vaynerchuk did not stop there. He also put the attention on the vintners he profiled, helping them build their businesses as well.

Still, those who enjoy social media glory will meet with their share of detractors, as Vaynerchuk told the *Times*: "Many people who I respected were disappointed when I started *Wine Library TV*. They thought I was dumbing down wine." An entrepreneur must address detractors like these—and truly, any critics, whether they make a valid point or not—and do so as quickly as possible, in order to prevent the kind of reputation jab that United Airlines endured when an irate passenger who had his prize guitar destroyed used YouTube to disparage United's customer service.

I follow this mantra with my own online show. Called *Basso On Business*, it is a program dedicated to helping companies solve the challenges they regularly face. While I receive mostly positive feedback, I do get occasional comments from viewers who criticize the business owners I profile, wondering what possessed me to believe these entrepreneurs ran good enough businesses to earn a spot on my show. I take all comments seriously, but not personally. I thank these viewers for their response, and I mention that I will keep an eye out to see if any of the allegations they raise turn out to be true. We have since expanded the site and now offer a DVD series to help businesses solve challenges, leadership initiatives, and we even have a fitness component, www.MyBusyFit.com, to help professionals keep their bodies as healthy as their organizations. Business, body, and mind is our overall philosophy.

Social media are an accessible and ever-growing forum for effective two-way communication. Remember, it is not acceptable to simply read a comment and let it sit, no matter how positive or negative. Each comment warrants a careful response. Trust me—your reputation depends on it.

> ### Entrepreneurial Insight
>
> If your website generates comments, do not let them sit. Address them all, even if they are negative.

Results, Results, Results

While many of us are meticulous about image, it's reputation—the meat behind the image—that matters most, as Jeff Hoffman told me. As you may recall, Hoffman built an IT company while he was a student at Yale without knowing anything about programming. Yet he could hire the expertise of reputable people who could write software, and could therefore deliver the kind of product his clients needed. He managed to build a roster of satisfied customers, and he made sure he served them well. As Hoffman accurately points out, "Track records buy you credit for one more shot. It takes you a lifetime to build a reputation, and one failure to crash. I was aware that reputation is the most valuable asset you'll ever have."

Maybe it was the confidence that Hoffman projected that initially won clients over, but it was his commitment to deliver that brought results. And those results build the best kind of reputation.

Confidence. Results. Reputation. These are all part of Hoffman's instinct, and what he looks to when making deals today. "There are times when I have left money on the table and walked away from deals I didn't feel good about," Hoffman says. This kind of approach has only increased his integrity capital. "Investors call me and say, 'Are you working on anything? Because you worked hard to earn our trust, and you delivered.'" Hoffman adds, "That's the gold in this game."

To win over the stakeholders, Hoffman says, you have to have confidence and believe in it. "Be swift and decisive," he advises. "Will you get every decision right every time? No. But then make corrections early. Nobody wants to hear that you don't know what you're doing. Figure out what you need to do, and do it."

Entrepreneurial Insight

Live up to your word. Don't promise anything that will leave stake-holders waiting for you to make good.

Of course, it helps to do your homework, as entrepreneurs are known to do. They zero in on what to read, whom to contact, what to ask, whom to meet, and whom to persuade to come on board, all in the name of moving forward and sealing deals.

When Honesty and Integrity Rule

Joe Corcoran likes to keep his word. So he was straightforward with audiences and investors alike whenever he talked about his show, *Tony and Tina's Wedding*, especially in terms of its unfamiliar audience-participation concept. In essence, the members of the audience interact with the cast and are treated like wedding guests. In fact, they are privy to gossip about the bride or groom. Corcoran's approach paid off, especially during the show's early days when he worked so hard to build a following. "People always knew me as a promoter," he says. "It fizzles down to my integrity and the fact that I was always honest. When I said it would be a great party, people trusted me, and they weren't disappointed. They left the show raving about it."

That tactic also helped Corcoran attract talent for the show, including people with star power such as baseball great Lee Mazilli. Mazilli came on board when he retired from playing and before he went on to coach the New York Yankees with Joe Torre. When someone like this joined the cast, news cameras and reporters followed, building more buzz for the show.

Yet Corcoran explains that he wasn't simply focused on crafting an image. "I was more concerned with treating people with respect, being honest, and acting with integrity," he says. "I had to make tough decisions that had the potential to make some people unhappy, but I always made sure to be accessible so that everyone could let me know how they felt. And I earned respect from people with whom I've worked and who work for me."

By actively listening to his stakeholders, Corcoran proved his character. Simply taking the time to remain accessible can make all the difference in winning people's trust and, as a result, their loyalty.

Trust Is Everything

Universal Music Publishing Group executive Evan Lamberg believes that trust goes a long way, even in an industry considered one of the most cutthroat. "The most valuable thing anyone owns is reputation," he states. "Human engagement only happens if trust is there. Artists will share new work with you and come to you with problems. I'm dealing with incredible musicians and artists whose songs are heard all over the globe. They need to know I'm dealing with them fairly."

When there is earned trust—from the artists to the executives to the interns—everything else tends to fall into place. "Not that I handle everything perfectly," Lamberg says. "I still have to make an effort to follow up, to call and work things out."

Trust, Lamberg says, is the only way to make it in the music field. "You can't be sustainably successful without a great reputation," he points out. "You can disagree with someone in the harshest way, but you've got to have a great reputation to go the distance because everything comes out of that."

Getting to Know You

Perhaps the best way to build your credibility is to get to know as many people as possible in a meaningful way. This strategy proved golden for Broadway and off-Broadway producer Ken Davenport, who rose to prominence in an industry in which he initially had no connections. Early in his career, Davenport tried to be in as many places, as often as he could, in order to learn as much as possible, and also to project himself as the doer he knew he was. "When people needed something, I was there," he says. "They'd say, 'Type this script up.' 'Drive this here.' I'd do anything. I wish I'd done it more, and put myself in it more." As Davenport has demonstrated, it's not just who you know, but who knows you—and what exactly they know and like about you—that can breed success.

Entrepreneurial Insight

Never be afraid to start at the bottom. This is perhaps one of the most organic ways to build meaningful relationships as you make your way in your industry, whatever it happens to be.

Not Just for Newbies

You must fine-tune your image and reputation continually, even after you have opened doors and built connections with influencers. Like other entrepreneurs, Scott Snibbe—the head of Snibbe Interactive—has seen the importance of image and reputation evolve over time. While his focus was at one time entirely on art and research—images that were at once cutting edge, experimental, and rebellious in nature—he is now called to project himself differently as CEO of a company with up to 20 employees.

"It's been a challenge as CEO," he notes. "I love the friendships with artists and researchers, the peer-to-peer, the when and how to get things done. But as the CEO, you're really the boss. I'm friendly with staff, but you have to be the visionary as well."

He continues: "I try to be compassionate. That's one of my favorite qualities about myself, but this job requires me to be firm, confident, even project a sense of threat. I'm in control of the business and people's jobs."

For Snibbe, the role is almost parental, and being a good parent does not necessarily always allow him to be the child's—or in this case, the employee's—friend. "When I move too much toward being friends, it means I'm doing a worse job as CEO," Snibbe points out. "My staff needs to have confidence in me. It's probably the biggest challenge. The CEO is a more conservative role, even though it's risky."

Entrepreneurial Insight

Effective entrepreneurs know they must be able to lead and plan in order not only to grow a business, but also to inspire faith and trust from others.

Effective leaders also understand that they must demonstrate extreme confidence and the ability to manage a business. Entrepreneurs often find themselves pulled in numerous directions and required to play countless roles while running an organization, roles such as therapist, guidance counselor, mentor, and even referee. That is why it is so important to have a plan, a roadmap in which you set goals and objectives so that there is already a policy in place when you need to make a snap decision. This allows owners and their companies to prove that they are consistent, reliable, and trustworthy, enabling organizations to grow along with their people.

A good image and reputation are critical whether your business is just starting out or well established. With trust as a foundation, an entrepreneur has the tools to navigate challenges, especially when it comes to opening doors and maintaining relationships. And when stakeholders see you as dependable and resourceful, the best opportunities tend to find you. That is something we look at next, in Chapter 4.

Summary

Never before have image and reputation played such a critical role in business. Impressions can be cultivated in a flash in this digital age; now more than ever, winning confidence is key. The following things are vital to remember when building relationships:

- Do your homework before meeting with clients, prospects, vendors, new hires, and investors, and show up to meetings prepared.
- Demonstrate that you care about your stakeholders' success.
- It's okay to keep certain things—such as your relative newness to an industry—to yourself, so long as you know that you can go the distance for your prospect or client. But it is never acceptable to outright lie.
- Hone your staff's core competencies, and you'll know in advance where to turn if you need assistance.
- Respond to both positive and negative feedback. You never want your reputation to get away from you.
- Guard your track record. It could mean the difference in winning not only repeat customers but also repeat investors.
- Build relationships from the ground up and, along the way, be willing to assist wherever you might be needed. People remember favors and kindness, and may help you in a similar way in the future.
- As a business owner, cultivate your reputation as a leader in order not only to meet your goals but also to enable those around you to grow.

4

Is That a Leprechaun in Your Pocket, or
Are You Just Happy to See Me?

SOME PEOPLE CATCH all the breaks. They have the A-list contacts and the lucrative contracts, and they interact in the circles where they discover the best prospects. Are they on some improbable lucky streak? Or do they have an extraordinary sense of timing?

Perhaps it's a little bit of both. However, it isn't simply the mystical plays of luck behind every right place, right time scenario; instead, there has likely been a lot of groundwork done and long hours spent, not to mention willingness to regularly get outside the familiar, where we can open ourselves up to new spheres of opportunity. Indeed, you can create your own luck by positioning yourself in places where good turns happen. Who knows? There might be something to the notion that there's a moment when the stars and moon align, creating the so-called lucky break. Nevertheless, as Jeff Hoffman states, "Luck favors the prepared." I tend to agree.

Entrepreneurial Insight

Create your own luck by positioning yourself in places where good turns happen.

Running with the Winners

I learned fairly early in life that opportunities will bypass you unless you make yourself available. There is truth to that right place, right time mentality, and it is this: You have to be particular about the company you keep and the places you frequent. This became obvious to me back in 1993 when I was a junior at Hofstra University on Long Island. On the night of a school basketball game, during halftime, there was a contest with high stakes—one lucky student would get the chance to win a semester's tuition for shooting six three-pointers in 30 seconds. Out of all the students vying for this chance, I was picked. Suddenly I was in the center of the gym, taking shots as if my life depended on it. I made all six shots, and the crowd went absolutely nuts. Sheer luck? I'd say no. Yes, I was randomly selected, but I was also playing basketball for two hours every day, and I happened to have a darn good three-point shot. This is just one example of how vital it is to be prepared when the occasion to shine arises—that way you will accumulate more wins than losses. I still have a copy of the school newspaper with a picture of me and some friends on the cover.

Entrepreneurial Insight

Don't wait for opportunities, make them happen.

This mantra became even more apparent to me when I discovered my future business partner at Advantage, whom I met while I was working for a different payroll company. Looking for new sales opportunities, I spent one day knocking on doors in Long Beach, New York. Never mind the "No Solicitors" sign in the windows; I had valuable information to share with the business inside. I entered an unassuming storefront and made my way to the receptionist. As it turned out, this particular business was a security company, so I figured I would not get in. They had cameras, door buzzers, and a tough little woman named Rose working the front desk. I made my best efforts to ask for the owner, trying to explain who I was and how my services benefitted small businesses just like this one. I tried to deliver my entire spiel before Rose threw me out. I was rebuffed. Undeterred, I asked Rose if she knew for sure that the owner would not see me—and just at that moment the owner chimed in from behind, saying, "Let him in." And lo and behold, I ended up signing him on as a new client during that visit.

Entrepreneurial Insight

When the gatekeeper turns you down, ask again if that person knows for sure that the decision maker won't see you.

I did not know it, but I had just met my future investor and business partner. Was it merely luck? Again, no. I was doing my job, and the opportunity was simply waiting for me to discover it. You make opportunities happen; they don't just simply appear.

At the Center of the Action

Luck is hard work and timing converging.
—Evan Lamberg, music publishing executive

For record executive Evan Lamberg, luck means being where the action is, and in the music industry that is largely New York. As a former pre-med student, Lamberg looked into a program his mother had discovered at New York University that would allow him to pursue a degree in music and business. He enrolled in the program for two reasons:

1. He liked it.
2. New York is a major center of the universe as far as music is concerned, and Lamberg liked being at the center of the universe. It was a given that the mega-deals transpired in New York City, not Albany.

Lamberg has felt a certain way about luck ever since he tried to break into the competitive music field. He says, "Luck is the result of hard work and timing converging. It's being in the environment where the breaks happen." Lamberg could not get enough of the music industry. He saw one side depicted through the MTV lens, but that told only one part of the story as far as he was concerned. More than anything, he wanted to know about the business and finance end of music. He wanted to see how a label turned a profit. He found out that there were internships at key companies through NYU. So he started knocking on doors, landing internships, and learning everything that he could. Lamberg went on to live and breathe the industry, happy in it and finding success. He built key relationships with upcoming artists, including Matchbox Twenty front man Rob Thomas. Lamberg found he enjoyed his work so much that there were times he was surprised to receive a bonus or paycheck; he was having that good a time.

> ### Entrepreneurial Insight
>
> A good way to make luck happen: Knock on doors.

Lamberg put himself in the right place at right time. If there was any luck anywhere in this scenario, it was that back in his college days, his mother, wanting nothing more than that her son should find happiness in his work, found this program at NYU, gave him the phone number, and told him to call and learn more.

"If my mother did not do that research, there's a pretty good chance I'd have finished at Albany and gone on to med school," Lamberg concedes. "I'd probably have been happy. But she turned the corner for me." For Lamberg, maybe the luck was being raised in a family that had the time and interest to help him understand his passions and lead him to a path where his dreams and success could be combined.

And when you are happy in work, Lamberg points out, your energy level is higher, you work longer hours, and you are more inspired. What about the paycheck? Lamberg says this: "It's like, oh my God, I'm getting paid for this? I would do this for nothing, which I did for years after college, interning and taking part-time jobs."

I'd gotten to know Lamberg shortly after he became a payroll client of mine; he ran a small entity that he owned while also working as a music executive. At the time, I was trying to help a musician get started, something I had mentioned to an attorney friend of mine. As it turned out, he had a music business friend to contact—and that person, coincidentally, was Lamberg, my client. Lamberg agreed to meet me and listen to the CD I brought along. Surrounded by stacks of CDs that also probably demanded his attention, Lamberg spent two hours with me listening to each song on my artist-friend's CD and sharing on-the-money industry insights. And even though Will Hawkins—the artist with whom I was working—did not get a record contract signed, I have great memories from working with him during the process.

Was I lucky to have this kind of access to someone whose help I needed at just that time? Maybe. But had I not opened my mouth and asked for contacts, I would have spun my wheels. "Luck"—however it's defined—pops up its head when you throw hesitancy aside and ask for a favor, one that may well end up helping the person whose advice you are seeking by way of new prospects. It doesn't hurt to help luck along by paving the road ahead with the opening, "Your opinion means a lot to me." Opportunity tends to follow.

Entrepreneurial Insight

"Luck"—however it's defined—pops up its head when you throw hesitancy aside and ask for that favor.

Boosting Those Odds

I used to tell people I have a leprechaun, and that sometimes the luck happened because I was standing where the leprechaun was standing.
—Jeff Hoffman, cofounder and CEO in the
Priceline.com family of companies

Jeff Hoffman is not one to scoff at luck. "I will take luck anytime it presents itself," he says. Not one to rely on luck alone, Hoffman also keeps both feet on the ground. "The difference is that all luck does is open doors when you're walking by. It's what you do with that luck—how well prepared you are—when luck shines."

Hoffman is the kind of serial entrepreneur who has enjoyed repeated success. As such, he knows that some people think he just stumbles into luck. "I used to tell people I have a leprechaun," he says with a laugh, "and that sometimes the luck happened because I was standing where the leprechaun was standing." But Hoffman was always in it to win, whatever the challenge. Never mind luck; hard work trumps it almost every time.

To shed light on this theory, Hoffman shares a tale—what he calls a goosebumps moment—about one of his friends, professional boxer Evander Holyfield. On one occasion, Hoffman stuck around at the gym where both men worked out while Holyfield trained for a fight.

"He's doing three sets of 100 things," Hoffman says. "And I'm counting 299 or 300. I say 300, he does one more. Holyfield says, 'The difference between 299 and 300 is the difference between being the heavyweight champ of the world and every other boxer. I can't stop and say that's good enough. If I quit at 299, someone else is staying up to do 300. Even if I'm tired, I'm going to finish it. Nobody else sees it.'"

In business, it pays to go the Evander Holyfield route. This is a lesson I learned back when I foot-canvassed for new clients when I worked in sales before becoming a business owner. I was especially tired and cold at the end of one wintry afternoon, and told myself I'd handed out enough business cards for the day. But I decided to go the extra mile anyway, and I entered a building without any regard to the "No Solicitors" sign. Riding up the elevator, I started chatting with a conservatively dressed man carrying an oversized briefcase.

"You must be an accountant," I said to him with an appreciative smile. "Either that, or an attorney."

"I'm an accountant," he said.

So, I asked where he was headed. And when he replied that he was on his way to a brokerage firm, I had to laugh, saying, "That's where I'm going. Can you introduce me?" He agreed—and I was on my way to signing on a new client.

The day's work didn't stop there. I spent evenings licking envelopes for mailers to new prospects while I sat in front of the television. My coworkers thought I was crazy, and my boss muttered frequently about my extra marketing expenses. No matter. Soon enough, I ranked number one in sales.

Entrepreneurial Insight

When it comes to preparation, go the extra mile. Do one more rep. It will help set you apart from everyone else.

Perseverance and the Lessons Gained

I had opportunity to make a lot of mistakes and recover from them.
—Joe Corcoran, coproducer of the long-running
off-Broadway show *Tony and Tina's Wedding*

Ask Joe Corcoran about his two-decade-plus run of *Tony and Tina's Wedding*, and he will tell you he was lucky. He will also say this: "I had opportunity to make a lot of mistakes and recover from them." He learned a lot from those mistakes; they taught him lessons he shares now with the show's producers in other cities to help them improve their luck. "We tried everything imaginable to make the show a success," Corcoran notes. Some of those ideas benefitted the show, while others did not. So, in order to keep the momentum of success, Corcoran now tells other producers exactly what succeeds and what doesn't. "I'll say, 'We tried that in New York, and it didn't work.' And I'll tell them why. Maybe the kind of ad they want to run is way too expensive. Or I'll explain, 'When we put ads in the *New York Times*, it didn't make a difference.'"

Throughout the *Tony and Tina* run, Corcoran and his team kept pushing, especially in the beginning when his organization ran the production on a shoestring, with zero dollars to spend on advertising. As Corcoran puts it, "You could say a person was in the right place at the right time, but underneath that is someone who worked very hard. Success isn't possible without perseverance. People get lucky, but they prepare for it. Luck is on the surface. Create your own luck on your experience and learn from your mistakes."

From the very beginning, Corcoran remained acutely aware that his audience was there to have a good time, and the show had to deliver. It was the show's burden to bear, which it did by sharing small, albeit profound, moments with the audience. Those small moments were like seeds that led to bigger payoffs. Corcoran recalls one night when Joan Rivers, whose husband had passed away, attended a performance. Mrs. Vitale, playing the bride's mother and a recent widow, approached Rivers. "They shared a special conversation, just the two of them, and Joan Rivers walked away, saying something like, 'You would not believe the conversation I just had.'"

Was it luck that brought Joan Rivers into the theater that night? Perhaps. But the intelligence of an insightful actor who seized that moment was also at play. She knew just what to say, and she appealed to the best kind of influencer. Perhaps that had less to do with luck and more to do with Corcoran's ability to build a team where members share the same mission. Here, the mission was to connect with the audience one-on-one, even in a roomful of people.

Entrepreneurial Insight

Build a team of talented and loyal players who can spot a lucky break as it happens and run with the opportunity to make it meaning-ful for your organization.

But Sometimes You Gotta Believe

Like most entrepreneurs, Mike Ireland likes a good opportunity. But he says opportunities rarely present themselves at the right time. And when they do, well, *that's* luck.

Ireland and his brother Russ are second-generation owners of the upscale Martin Viette Nurseries, a tony garden center on Long Island's north shore, whose expertise is often showcased during the renowned Macy's Flower Show at Herald Square. In 2009, the Martin Viette nursery opened a satellite store at the Americana Manhasset, a luxury shopping center along a destination known as the Miracle Mile. And sales continue to be strong.

Granted, not many retailers could have landed this opportunity, given what many consider premier real estate no matter the state of the economy. As Ireland explained, the property owner approached the Martin Viette nursery with the suggestion that a satellite store would be a great mix among a lineup that includes high-end retail names like Coach, Chanel, and Gucci. But that is not where luck comes into play. Ireland has known the owner of the Americana since he was a teenager, so the old adage was at play: Do business with the people you trust, whose products you like, and whose reputation is top notch. Luck appeared when the retailer right next to Tiffany's closed, providing the opportunity for Martin Viette to move in.

Entrepreneurial Insight

Do business with people you know, and they will think of you first when they come across an opportunity that may give your operation a boost.

"The lucky part was the location," Ireland says. "We could have been in the back corner. For us the luck opened up because the store is right next to Tiffany's, and the luxury market is picking up. What's helping us thrive is that we're different from the other shops there. We're not a clothing retailer or jewelry store."

Luck, Ireland explains, also played a role when his father ran the business during the 1970s. At the time, he was looking to relocate his operation onto about an acre of land, and instead he found a business on 42 acres whose owner was looking to sell. That spot has been home to Ireland's company ever since.

Think about it: Is Ireland's success the outcome of luck or what happens to those who cultivate relationships over time?

Visibility

We hear stories about lucky breaks, such as when a young singer named Justin Bieber was discovered because of his video postings on YouTube. Arguably, those kinds of moments are rare, but that does not mean you can't become visible to influencers who can make a difference. When you do good work and are recognized by your peers—and have helpful tools like the Internet and search engines to broadcast a good reputation—people tend to notice.

> **Entrepreneurial Insight**
>
> Broadcast your company's good news everywhere. You never know which influencers are paying attention.

That was the case for Ari Fish, a *Project Runway* contestant from Kansas City, Missouri. There was no right-place, right-time scenario that led her to audition, Fish says. Rather, the show found her. "I received an e-mail to apply by one of their casting agents that were scouting the 'talent,'" she notes. "I was informed that the deadline had been extended and they urged me to apply. At first it was a bit of a joke, but the idea ran through my veins, and I reread the e-mail aloud, and it was then I knew that if I did apply, I would get on."

Although Fish—whom *Runway* judge and renowned fashion consultant Tim Gunn described as "deeply conceptual"—was voted off the show early in the season, she did go on to win cash-prize competitions, and she kept her name in the media for her avant-garde designs. She likens the *Project Runway* experience to playing with fire. "Sometimes when you play with fire, you get burned," she notes. "And if you're lucky, you realize that as soon as you extinguish one fire, another has started somewhere else. This is what I learned from *Project Runway*."

I encountered a bit of this frenetic pace myself when I auditioned for season two of *The Apprentice*. My publicist pressed me to do it, thinking it would be good for business. I was reluctant at first—how could I be on the show and run my business?—yet I, along with 5,000 others, went to an open casting call, and I even got a callback. I not only began to see myself on the show; I saw myself winning. Sitting in the boardroom with "The Donald" did not scare me. Hell, I was on trial every day running a business. Even though I did not make it beyond the second round, I knew that this didn't make me any less of a businessperson. In fact, I felt lucky to have played a role in the show's second season. It bolstered my feelings of striving for success, and because I got a taste of the show's production, it planted the seeds for my own show, *Basso On Business*.

Entrepreneurial Insight

Take the occasional step way outside your comfort zone. You may wind up discovering new and refreshing directions that could help you grow your organization.

Front and Center

Steve Davies, a New York management consultant and former head of US Computer Group, made certain he was in the right place at the right time by keeping his company in the spotlight. "I entered every awards program that I could—the *Inc.* 500, the crowning glory, Ernst and Young Entrepreneur of the Year; I applied for everything."

His firm reaped in the accolades and was the only firm to place on the LPMG/Long Island Business News 25 Fastest-Growing Companies on Long Island for eight consecutive years. "The visibility that comes as a result of winning these awards was enormous," Davies says, adding that the judges audited the firm's financials, providing his firm a highly respected level of integrity.

"My whole marketing strategy was about third-party endorsements, underlining the stature of the company," Davies explains. It meant constant ceremonies and events attended by key decision makers of prospects and clients, at which Davies was front and center.

Entrepreneurial Insight

Business award ceremonies are fantastic venues for meeting the real captains of industry in your field.

Still, a lot of strategic planning went into situating the company in a way that made Davies and his team stand out in a crowd. That included diversifying the client base. "I saw a lot of businesses that existed because they had one or two large contracts," he says. "We had just under 3,000 small customers each paying $6,000 a year. But we also had Citibank and Bear Stearns."

In addition, he says, many competing firms were run by technicians who started their companies because they were skilled IT professionals. Davies, a former banker, entered the field from a different perspective. "I was focused on the business aspect of it. I took a lot of small contracts away from larger competitors that they didn't care about. They woke up one morning and saw I'd taken $3 million in business. By then it was too late."

"The harder you work, the luckier you get," Davies says. "I don't think I'm a particularly lucky person. It's about positioning, and sometimes you get the lucky breaks, in my opinion; you think luck happens to someone else."

Winning might seem lucky, but there's no lottery element to the competitions Davies entered. His every move was very tactical; it was more like a game of chess than a game of chance.

The harder you work, the luckier you get.
—Steve Davies, Founder of US Computer Group

A Higher Calling

For some, of course, growing a business has less to do with luck than it does with a higher presence. Take Selena Cuffe, the founder of Heritage Link Brands, an organization that educated US consumers about the wines of South Africa and its diaspora—a matter she found to be grossly unrepresented.

Cuffe came up with the idea for the company during her travels to Johannesburg when she stopped by a wine festival. "I believe in the grace of God more than luck," she says. "I was at a wine tasting and asked a lot of questions in South Africa; I think it was more than luck. There were other people at that wine festival who didn't quit their jobs and launch this business."

But for Cuffe, the chance to empower black South African wine growers was too important a cause to dismiss. "To change people's perception of Africa, I had a talk with God," she says. "It's bigger than wine."

Call it positive thinking. Call it luck, or even the power of prayer. Good things happen to those who align their beliefs with their actions. There is no question that faith can fortify a person. But without an action plan, the chance for success is slim. Of course, it also helps to dream big, an essential element we will look at next.

Entrepreneurial Insight

Good things happen to those who align their beliefs with their actions.

Summary

Even if you are a true believer in luck, it can never hurt to give luck an extra boost by positioning yourself in the spots where people tend to catch the big breaks. That means extending your circle, staying informed, and asserting yourself so that you are in the presence of decision makers. Put yourself among the lucky ones with these strategies in mind:

- Vie for opportunities. Someone will come out the winner; it might as well be you.
- Try to get around the gatekeepers.
- Knock on doors, and knock again. Each new open door will lead you closer to the kind of break that will help you grow your business.
- Put yourself where the stars in your industry gather. It is easier to catch a break when you are in the center of the action.
- Make sure you are in an industry that makes you happy. This is the best way to stay inspired. Remember, people like to do business with positive people.
- Throw hesitancy aside. You are much less likely to encounter luck if you are too reticent to ask for advice or assistance.
- Encourage luck by being prepared for whatever endeavor you decide ultimately to pursue.
- When preparing, go beyond that extra mile to stay miles ahead of your competition.
- Ask for introductions. People generally like to help.
- Broadcast the good work that you do; you never know which influencers are paying attention.
- Don't be afraid to try something new, even if it seems a bit foreign to you. It always helps to widen your horizons and discover new opportunities.
- A great place to network with the A-list crowd is awards galas. Might as well run with the winners.
- Figure out where your competitors are dropping the ball, and then one-up them. You will win new market share, strategically creating your own luck.
- Back up your belief in luck or faith with a powerful action plan to score big wins.

5

Foster Bold Dreams, Bolder Actions

WHAT SETS THE wildly successful person apart from everyone else? Well, there are a few things: imagination, a solid plan of action, and serious determination to break down barriers. In order to win big, you need all three.

That's not to say that you need to pinpoint early on exactly what you plan to do. For many of us, figuring that out is part of a fantastic journey. And we're not satisfied unless we challenge ourselves to determine how to achieve what others might dismiss as long shots. Call it the difference between true entrepreneurs and complacent business people.

Yet even the most self-assured should not try to go at it alone. It always helps to have someone in your corner—whether that's a partner, a spouse, or a mentor—someone who can help you learn from your mistakes, or guide you in preparing for what could be an incredible adventure.

Sure, this kind of journey might keep you awake at night, but for those who enjoy the ride, it provides the kind of gratifying fun we used to experience as kids, back when we had time to dream and knew little about struggling to surmount obstacles. In fact, in some cases, our vivid childhood imaginations gave us the sustenance to feed some of our adult accomplishments, regardless of how specific or vague our ambitions.

Take Priceline cofounder Jeff Hoffman, who—with his computer science degree from Yale University—spent some time working in the aerospace industry in Cape Canaveral, Florida. He had a job as an engineer, writing software for space shuttle launches. When asked about his childhood, Hoffman says, "I was a stereotypical little guy. I was fascinated with the unknown and exploration. I went through an astronaut phase. Later, I made friends with real astronauts. I always thought about doing something with my life that would allow me to see the world." Hoffman, now a world traveler whose success in business has given him the freedom to see 60 countries, says the possibility of failure has never been enough of a reason to thwart his dreams. "I was always fascinated by technology," he says. "I tried to build

71

a robot, and was determined to make it work, even if I had zero percent chance of actually doing so."

What captured Hoffman's imagination—even beyond space exploration—was the independence that is so inherent in entrepreneurship. "It was never about money, but freedom," Hoffman says about his burning quest to make it as an entrepreneur and call the shots to realize all of his dreams. And he wasn't going to achieve any of these dreams stuck in a cubicle.

Of course, you increase your odds of making it work when you mix imagination, follow-up, and perseverance. In almost all cases, that's the winning combination for success.

Have a Résumé with that Sandwich

Twenty-somethings may be young, attractive, and ready to take on anything when they enter the workforce. But real-world savvy? Not so much. If they're smart, they put the power of their imaginations to work for them as they begin to define themselves in the workplace, and the sooner they do so, the better.

This is something I learned for myself upon graduating from Hofstra University with a BA in history and education. I was eager to begin a long and rewarding teaching career, only to find out that school districts were not hiring. To make ends meet, I found myself begging for my old college job back, slinging sandwiches at a local deli in an office park.

I was not afraid of hard work, but I had envisioned myself postgraduation on the other side of the counter, ordering the sandwiches rather than making them. Fortunately, the deli owners agreed to rehire me. And because they were kind enough to recognize that sandwich making was not in my long-term future, they allowed me to fit job hunting into my workday. They cut me some slack when I began promoting myself at work by wrapping my résumé with every sandwich order I prepared, waiting for customer reactions. (I can still picture people pushing the mustard aside to get a glimpse of my résumé underneath.) I was marketing and didn't even really know it. In all fairness, some of the customers did not respond favorably; yet I kept at it, undeterred and encouraged by those who invited me to interview. In fact, that's ultimately how I landed my first job in the payroll industry.

> **Entrepreneurial Insight**
>
> Want to get noticed? Market yourself to your desired audience, even if they don't expect it.

Less than a year later, I was wooed by another company, Advantage Payroll, a firm that wanted to expand on Long Island. They presented the following offer to me: I'd start out as an employee, with the opportunity to buy a license agreement and run an independent office. There was no guarantee they would let me buy it; it was a let's-wait-and-see-what-you-do kind of thing. Still, I was determined. I had the chance at the tender age of 24 to become a business owner. All I had to do was sign up clients and somehow raise enough money to purchase the license. It couldn't be hard, right?

Six months later, I turned to Marty, the man from the security company whom I had signed on as a client right on the spot, and who was my best customer. I knew he had a successful business and was not risk averse. He had already taken a chance on me when purchasing the previous service and was pleased with the results I delivered, so I figured it was a good place to start. What did I have to lose?

I called Marty and told him about my plans. I then presented him with a well thought out business proposal that my father and I had spent most of our spare time preparing. It required very little negotiation to get Marty to agree to loan me the money in return for a stake in the business. I can remember standing in the rain to sign our partnership agreement on the back of his BMW, a vehicle I most certainly coveted, on Bell Boulevard in Bayside, Queens. Never mind the rain. I was on my way.

> **Entrepreneurial Insight**
>
> If you're big on dreams and short on cash, seek out an investor who has confidence in you. But write a really good business plan first.

Surround Yourself with Believers

Surround yourself with people who can help you take risks.
                    —Evan Lamberg, music publishing executive

For some people, the taste of possibilities starts early. Evan Lamberg, who has represented some of the most popular artists in the music industry, always loved reading about the music business, even as a kid. Couple that innate fascination with people who foster the determination for success, and the result is an inner resolve that's hard to beat. "I grew up in a nurturing family, with parents who said, 'If you can dream it, and work hard at it, you can get it done,'" Lamberg notes. "My parents supported whatever I could imagine doing as a child."

Lamberg has looked for those qualities in the people in his circle today, whether it's his parents' continued presence, his wife, or his associates. "You don't succeed 100 percent on your own," he says. "Surround yourself with people who can help you take risks. I don't spend my time with people who say I can't do something." Still, yes-men need not apply. "I surround myself with people who have opposing points of view and who see things differently than I do," Lamberg points out. "I like people with imagination, but one that challenges and makes you see things in a more constructive way."

Yet despite these opposing points of view, Lamberg's close friends and associates still had to be believers. One of his key supporters was record executive Martin Bandier, who took Lamberg under his wing in the early 1990s. That was when Lamberg was just getting started in the business. Bandier took a liking to Lamberg and began teaching him not only how to achieve success, but also how to cope with failure.

Lamberg told me about a deal that he had pushed hard to win, had it in his hands, and then in the final hour blew it. Bandier took the young Lamberg aside and said something along the lines of, "The bad news? You lost the deal. The good news? You learned from this. A couple of moves you made weren't right. You'll take it to the next deal. There will be one around the corner." It's a lesson Lamberg keeps in mind to this day. "Of course, you need a track record of making deals," he says. "But you can't learn without failure. Anyone who's never stumbled—that's not a person I want in my life."

Entrepreneurial Insight

Don't be afraid to make mistakes. Take heart in the fact that you will be better prepared for the next opportunity that comes your way.

Lamberg also points out that while nobody seeks to fail, there's no shame in doing so. In fact, the experience can be liberating. "To this day, when I have a day go by and I haven't failed at something, big or small, I haven't learned how to do something better."

As Lamberg says, sometimes the best way to ensure that you keep learning is to continue putting yourself in an atmosphere where you're apt to fail. Taking measured risks is perhaps the best way to stretch your entrepreneurial chops. That said, it's key to surround yourself with mentors who can guide you to adjust your course when needed.

Everyday Case Study/To Facebook or Not to Facebook

Subject business: Catz Fitness Franchisee, Commack, NY

View Video at: www.BassoOnBusiness.com

Catz Fitness of Commack, New York, is run by serial entrepreneur Adam Zeitsif and his partner, Dr. Bill Germano, a successful chiropractor. They joined forces based on Adam's business prowess and Bill's natural affinity to health and wellness. After originally specializing in training competitive athletes, they made a decision to branch out and include individuals looking to live a healthier lifestyle along with their young children. Today Adam and Bill not only help many former couch potatoes to live a more active lifestyle, but also have developed a strong base with high school athletes aiming to take fitness to the next level.

(continued)

(*continued*)

Catz's challenges started mounting shortly after Adam and Bill built their world-class facility in Commack. They were struggling to get the word out to the local market about what Catz training was capable of. Since Catz was not a household name and had a significantly larger presence on the west coast, their marketing efforts had to be more robust than they originally anticipated. Further complicating matters, Adam and Dr. Germano insisted that the only way you could truly see how effective Catz training really was would be to experience it firsthand. That meant they had to get human beings in the door, right? Maybe.

As we toured the facility, complete with an Astroturf indoor field, my team realized that Adam and Dr. Germano truly had a unique spin on fitness. The building was oddly devoid of muscle-building equipment, such as free weights and weight machines, as well as the standard selection of treadmills and recumbent bicycles. Instead, the facility featured a large open space for a battery of almost military style drills that used mostly a person's own body weight and other one-of-a-kind equipment. It was clear why they wanted people to see their impressive facility in person.

The duo quickly received endorsements from the region's professional lacrosse team and boasted a modest enrollment of new candidates based on the print media and mailings they were doing. However, this still was not filling their facility and ambitions to their capacity. My team and I probed a bit, asking questions about their social media campaign. Adam and Dr. Germano stated they had just recently created their Facebook account. Enter social media and public relations.

Catz features an innovative and fresh approach to fitness; they needed to reinvent their marketing strategy to reflect this. The Basso On Business team devised an innovative strategy that harnessed the power of video to showcase their abilities and let the community see how truly unique Catz training is (http://www.youtube.com/watch?v=41BMGmtRIzY). With the advent of video you can truly expand the possibilities of your business and change the buying paradigm to work within the new set of rules that is emerging in our culture. Video can bring to life your vision of a product or service in a controlled environment allowing you to create the exact tone or feeling you want your message to elicit. Through short video posts on their website and their expanded selection of social media platforms, Adam and Dr. Germano deliver riveting snippets of their workouts to their online fan base and beyond. They also reached out to current clients and asked them to write a review of their experience at Catz. These videos, combined with online testimonials from satisfied clients, helped to drive new traffic through Catz's doors.

We also suggested that Adam and Dr. Germano use a public relations firm to get the word out through regional news outlets in order to be showcased as experts in their field, not as an advertiser in a publication. They have done a wonderful job at capturing the attention of the local and regional press in publications that work well for their industry. We are thrilled with the progress they have made bolstering their stature as a fitness leader in the region.

The work does not stop once you post a few things on Facebook and get yourself in some publications. Information and reviews become stale. You need to set aside specific time to work on these initiatives and create a budget to use these tools effectively to create new content that is relevant to your audience. Catz Fitness of Commack realizes this and works hard to ensure that they keep the information they provide both relevant and exciting. While they have not yet reached their aspiration of a packed facility, they are well on their way, and I am certain that with their continued efforts they will soon achieve their goal.

SUMMARY

- Understand your uniqueness and showcase it proudly.
- Use social media (Facebook, Twitter, LinkedIn, etc.) to support your brand efforts.

(*continued*)

> (*continued*)
>
> ■ Public relations are an important piece of any business. Just pick up the phone and call a reporter—they are literally waiting for a good story.
> ■ The work is never really over. Keep content fresh, relevant, authentic, and entertaining.
>
> Information taken from a personal interview with Adam Zeitsif and Dr. Bill Germano on October 30, 2009; video © Basso On Business.

Pace Yourself!

Fail enough times, and perhaps you'll learn to right the ship in order to avoid the total collapse of your business. Just ask Steve Davies, former head of US Computer Group. Under Davies's leadership, the company won all sorts of prestigious national accolades and was continually recognized for its fast growth. That's no surprise, given Davies's outlook. "Growing up," says Davies, who was born and raised in England, "I was always ambitious. I joined Barclays Bank and thought I'd end up running it or being at the very top of it."

Yet Davies wound up settling in New York and growing his IT startup, US Computer Group. As is the case with most savvy entrepreneurs, Davies, a natural marketer, hired others to do what he couldn't do himself, including sales and IT. Perseverance worked in his favor. "I never give up," he says. "I never take no for an answer or accept the status quo. If someone thinks it has to be one way, I keep pushing and finding other ways to do things."

Entrepreneurial Insight

Follow your heart and interests, even if they are way outside the path that you originally expected to take.

One thing Davies always pushed for was business growth. "I'd ask the vice president how much can we grow the top line, and he'd roll his eyes. I'd ask, 'What resources do you need?' He'd say another telemarketer and two more salesmen." And Davies would add the required staff.

That kind of growth requires capital. "I was creative in raising money," he explains. "I had a vision for where I wanted the company to be. We were going to do an IPO and be a $100 million company. We did a video in 1997 where we laid all that out. I should look at it now; it would be a good laugh."

The company grew too fast to sustain itself—providing the ultimate lesson learned. "I should have taken some time out and flattened the growth," Davies says, looking back now. A painful lesson, to be sure, but one that helps him advise his current clients for his New York management consultancy properly.

Temper, Temper

Although they are very ambitious, entrepreneurs are often frustrated when success does not seem to come quickly enough. When I first launched the Basso On Business brand, I was eager to start a television show that would help entrepreneurs achieve personal success. I wanted to reach the largest audience possible. Producers and industry experts told me it could take two to five years, if it even happened at all. This was a problem for me, because I am admittedly impatient and like to see immediate results. So I learned to temper my expectations and establish small goals that allow me to see some measure of success at the end of each week, whether it is an improvement to my website, my show's production, or the monthly Basso On Business event called "Working Lunch with Rob" that I host for entrepreneurs across the nation. By setting modest benchmarks, I feel better about each accomplishment along the way.

When the Sky's the Limit

Sometimes all you need to get started on your path to destiny is an open mind. Consider the case of Broadway and off-Broadway producer Ken Davenport, who loved theater as a kid and even auditioned for his first play at the young age of five. By the time he was a student at Johns Hopkins University in Baltimore, Maryland, he was all set to study law. Still, since he thought theater was so much fun, he decided to study acting so that he would have no regrets later in life about what could have been. After all, he could always return to studying law.

Davenport delved into theater, not just taking on acting roles but becoming involved in other aspects of theater as well. A production assistant position with My Fair Lady, starring Richard Chamberlain, opened his eyes to all the opportunities in theater. A speaker at NYU had said, "You'll all work in this business. You may not be in the position that you think you'll be right now. Follow the road where it takes you."

And that's exactly what Davenport did—follow every opportunity, all the way to the role of producer.

Second Generation: Making the Business Your Own

Entrepreneurial Insight

When taking over a family business, don't be afraid to move away from the old guard.

It's one thing to start and build a business from scratch. It's another thing entirely to take a family business and mold it to your vision while pushing for new potential. You might have to go against the grain; you definitely need to put in seriously long hours; and you can't go wrong with perseverance. Just ask Mike Ireland who, along with his brother Russ, took over the family business, an upscale Long Island retailer called Martin Viette Nursery, which had humble beginnings as a gardening and lawn maintenance center. I would personally recommend that Mike and Russ find a system that permits them to work fewer hours and spend more time focusing on delegating and leading the company vision. Spring had barely arrived when I spoke with Mike, and he was gearing up for 80-hour workweeks until Christmas. For him, those hours are spent gaining knowledge; he's learning everything he can, not only about gardening but also about visual merchandising and retailing. He's sharing his vision with his employees, and transforming his business into a destination for gardeners from all over Long Island and beyond. For Mike, the effort is hardly a chore. "I love it," he says. "I can't wait to get up and come to work every day. I dive in and learn everything I can, working hard. It's not 70 hours surfing the web, but diving in and helping your people."

As a result, the two brothers doubled the business their parents had started. But it took years, since the brothers worked their way up into management roles prior to taking the lead. As principals of the company, they recruited and hired, building their own team of workers who share in their vision and goals. As Mike puts it, by handpicking their team, "there is no baggage from a bygone time with people who think you had a silver spoon." They selected not only staffers but also professionals, from payroll to accounting to lawyers, "to move away from the old guard from my parents' generation." Those from the old guard, who'd grown "fat and happy because they thought my father would retain their services," were not pleased to discover their gig was up under Mike and Russ Ireland. In some cases, their father was none too pleased with the new direction. "But I did always have his support," Mike says. "My father knew it was on my shoulders."

Entrepreneurial Insight

Less than 33 percent of family businesses survive the transition from first to second generation, according to the US Small Business Administration. And of those that do survive that transition, almost half do not make it through the transition from second to third generation.

Mike Ireland's strategy was possibly the smartest approach he could have taken. Less than one-third of family businesses survive the transition from first to second generation, according to the US Small Business Administration. If you are taking over a family business, you have to make it your own; you cannot just blindly operate within the status quo. Change can be a good thing—and especially in a difficult economy, change may be the very thing a business needs for its own survival.

Are You Off Your Rocker?

New ideas require extraordinary vision.
—David Becker, president of Philippe Becker Design, Inc.

In order to move forward in business, it helps to add a healthy dose of perspective. For example, take David Becker, president of San Francisco branding and packaging agency Philippe Becker. Though Becker's firm is a small company with only 20 employees, Whole Foods liked the agency's work so much that they retained it to create their private label design for 365 Organics.

In his quest for business, Becker—also an avid skydiver—tends to keep his cool. "My attitude was, I've got nothing to lose," he says. "What's the worst that can happen? We won't get the business. Or the best? We *will* get the business. But I can't be afraid of what might happen."

Becker concedes that sharing ideas is risky, especially in an industry where he constantly must come up with creative solutions to a challenge. To maintain perspective, he thinks of innovators in history. Many of them, he points out, "were social outcasts until people realized years later they were right. It's interesting to see how all the great scientific breakthroughs—the world is not flat, or Einstein's theories—prompted people to violently oppose and assume that the individuals who suggested them were off their rocker. Sometimes these thinkers were even burned at the stake! It turned out it was human nature to trash new ideas because what this person is proposing doesn't fit it into your paradigm."

As Becker points out, if a new vision is too abstract, the average person sees no use for it. He adds that new ideas—especially those brought to fruition—require extraordinary vision. Prior to Microsoft's success, the idea of a billion-dollar software company probably sounded ludicrous. But not to Bill Gates, a measured guy with a plan and a vision. Without these qualities, an upstart faces the impossible.

So when presenting concepts for a new brand, whether it's conservative or an idea that pushes the envelope, Becker is very deliberate in sharing his vision and is careful not to alienate clients. After all, they are the ones paying for his recommendations and the passion of his convictions.

That perspective seems to give him an almost Zen-like stance: "I'm not a neurosurgeon, and I'm not a general where if I make a horrible mistake, a thousand people are going to die. What's the worst that can happen? I'll get their attention."

Nurturing Creativity

Entrepreneurial Insight

Find the space to nurture and grow your new pursuits.

While dreams may be well and good, they are sometimes not evolved fully enough to pay the rent. It's also critical to hold on to and make time for your dreams, as Scott Snibbe, of Snibbe Interactive, learned early on as he pursued his artistry while he was a student. While studying at Brown University and the Rhode Island School of Design, Snibbe learned he had to fit his artistic pursuits around his schoolwork. He carried this approach with him into the professional world, where he continued to work on his art. "As soon as we finished a big deadline, or whenever we finished a big demo, there'd be a one- or two-week grace period. I'd use that time to make something personal or meaningful and dive into my own projects," he says. "My attitude has always been that it's better to beg forgiveness than ask permission."

Snibbe would get one of his art projects far enough along to enter it into an exhibit and build interest. "Then I'd go to my boss and say I was invited to a show; that's the 'beg forgiveness' part. That's how I did my side projects that became my company. You need to find time."

Fitting creativity into what others don't consider work time can make all the difference, says Snibbe, citing author Umberto Eco as a role model for this strategy.

It's better to beg forgiveness than ask permission.
—Scott Snibbe, Snibbe Interactive

Revise When Necessary

Sometimes, of course, our dreams and plans may need revising—and more than once. Take Selena Cuffe, the CEO of Heritage Link Brands, which imports wines from South Africa. According to Cuffe, now a young mother, "I wanted to be a partner at Goldman Sachs and have six kids. I still want to have more kids. I interned at Goldman and worked for Merrill Lynch, and I thought, 'This is not fun.'"

But Cuffe knows that she's doing more than tapping into South Africa's $3 billion wine industry. "I feel like I'm changing the perception of Africa. There's a lot of ignorance. The continent is very diverse. It's ripe with opportunities to make money, grow and build, and do fabulous things." Perseverance, she says, plays a big role. "It's huge," she says. "There are plenty of times when I want to call it a night." Yet knowing her company is changing the wine industry in South Africa—and the fact that the work she does helps improve others' lives—fuels her as she moves forward. "It must be similar to being black in 1870," she points out. "There was a lot of ignorance of people thinking black people don't know how to run a business. Fighting for civil rights and equality—that's what keeps me going."

As Cuffe points out, having a plan B can make all the difference when it comes to finding true fulfillment and success. I see this in my own career path, having studied to be an educator, switched to entrepreneur, and kept that business growing while transitioning again into the entertainment industry with Basso On Business.

Yet just dreaming big is not enough. You need to figure out a way to entice others to embrace your new direction. It helps to have passion for your new path, as is the case with Cuffe. For me, it is the passion for an endeavor that enables entrepreneurs to achieve their personal success. In pushing forward with Basso On Business, I am tapping all my skill sets as an educator, communicator, and entrepreneur. More importantly, I am enjoying the ride so much and learning along the way.

Sometimes business success is easier than imagined. Most of the time, however, it's not. You need vision and a plan B, if not also a plan C and D. It also helps to be a scrapper. And there's another essential ingredient: grassroots strategies, which we investigate in Chapter 6.

Entrepreneurial Insight

Big dreams propel you forward when they are driven by entrepreneurial passion.

Summary

Any big dream worth pursuing deserves an equally big action plan, not to mention a healthy dose of imagination. Yet it is futile to expect that one person can do it all. In getting your big idea off the ground, keep the following in mind:

- Don't be afraid to promote yourself, especially if it's a format that you have not seen before.
- Find a supporter who can help you either as a mentor, investor, or both.
- Remember: while your supporters may play devil's advocate sometimes, this can help your idea become that much stronger.
- Take measured risks, so that if you fail, you are not in the precarious position of losing everything.
- Don't accept the status quo. Look for new ways to accomplish your goals.
- Set modest benchmarks so that you can see progress, even if it happens incrementally.

- When you love your work, you will wake up wanting to dive in on most days.
- If you are taking over your family business, make it your own. There is no reason to keep the old guard around if they are not delivering the kind of results you expect.
- Fit in the time to work on your big dreams. Look for quiet moments in your schedule when you can afford to indulge in your goals for your next venture.
- Be flexible, and turn on a dime if you need to in order to keep your dream alive.

6

Humble Beginnings

BOOTSTRAPPING ENTREPRENEURS VERY likely share one key quality: They are ever resourceful. They rely on their ingenuity, knowing there is always a way to get something done and done well without spending a lot of cash. And let's face it: Most of us lack deep pockets, especially during the start-up phase. Because we are not General Electric or Johnson & Johnson—at least not yet—we need to come up with creative ways to navigate our business challenges and keep the overhead low. Consider the start-ups that put an old, unwanted door across two chairs, instantly creating a desk rather than buying furniture. Or the owner who has a steady supply of capable freelancers she presents to clients as staff. Or the chef who whets the appetite of passersby by handing out samples. It's all part of this nonstop survival mode—figuring how to trump your competition, turn a profit, build a network of influencers, and sleep at night, knowing that we can make payroll not just this week, but next week too, and the week after that.

Many entrepreneurs are lucky enough to have a mentor or role model to help guide us. Most of us learn to sharpen our resourcefulness on the fly and charge forward in the meantime, putting ourselves where the action is. As music publishing executive Evan Lamberg notes, Woody Allen was spot-on when he said that 80 percent of success is just showing up. But, as Lamberg also knows, you need to do a whole lot more than simply show up to win in business; you also need to network and actively listen. In essence, you have to prove yourself. Grassroots strategies can be the most effective and inexpensive way to do so, especially when your business has humble beginnings.

Mom, You're Hired

Experts recommend keeping costs as low as possible when launching a business—something my business partner Marty understood completely. Marty was in his mid-fifties when I met him. I was in my early twenties at the time and had very little practical business experience, so I looked to Marty for guidance. Even though we frequently differed in opinion, Marty was generally right when it came to cost savings. For proof, all I needed to do was compare his million-dollar house to his meager office setting. Clearly, the man took his savings home, though he also managed to create a positive working environment for his staff. Following Marty's lead, I spent as little as possible on office space, purchasing only essential equipment including a good printer. I always tried to save money where I could. That is why I rented space in a commercial building's storage room, converting the area into a makeshift office. My desk was an old castaway from some other tenant, and there I worked surrounded by boxes and forgotten equipment from other occupants in the building. Glamorous it definitely was not. However, I didn't need to impress anyone with my professional setting; providers tend to visit clients in the payroll industry service, rather than the other way around. To protect my image, I made sure that nobody dropped by my office, ever. And when it came to staff, I hired my mom because she was available, inexpensive, and trustworthy.

Entrepreneurial Insight

When first starting out in business, spend as little money as possible, and only on the essentials.

Then I hit the pavement, from 7 AM to 9 PM almost daily, keeping company with accountants—influencers who I hoped would then recommend me to decision makers. I filled my days with networking, making cold calls, and inviting prospects and clients to lunches and seminars. With limited dollars, I had no advertising budget except to run an ad in the yellow pages. Instead, I relied on one-to-one marketing, which was both cheaper and more effective than advertising to the masses. I devoted time to prepare for client meetings so that I would be the most knowledgeable person in the room. No one was going to best me on the industry trends. After all, I wanted people to look to me as the expert. I was so eager to highlight my knowledge and persuade them to retain me to handle their payroll that I sometimes literally jumped out of my chair during client meetings to make my points. Looking back, I think people gravitated toward me because of my almost ridiculous enthusiasm. One new client actually asked my referral partner if I was on drugs. Nevertheless, I charged on, determined to get people to believe in me. The formula worked, and my client list was soon growing. Still, there were hardships. More than once a client was bought out, and the next thing I knew I was out as a vendor. Lesson learned: Diversify. I don't have a single client today who represents more than 3 percent of my revenue—a scenario that increases stability and makes it much less painful when a client leaves.

Entrepreneurial Insight

Travel with the influencers who can help you get to know decision makers.

Embed Yourself

Picture this. You want more than anything to work in the entertainment industry. And you'll do just about anything—ethics intact, of course—to break in. For you, being a part of the business is not a matter of if, but when. That was the scenario for Evan Lamberg. Commitment, however, is one thing; access is another beast entirely. And Lamberg had no access. New York University contacts aside, he knew no one in the field. No entrenched relatives with connections ready to make an introduction. If Lamberg were to break in, he knew all too well that he would have to do it on his own.

So when Lamberg secured an internship or a part-time job while he was an NYU student, he took the opportunity seriously. "One of my strategies was showing up really early," he reveals. "I was very diligent in seeing what people needed, and being emotionally intelligent, I'd reach out to the executives and say, 'Do you need help with that in some small way?'" Because Lamberg was at such a junior level, his request to help was usually declined. Lamberg persisted. "I'd say, 'What's that—a pile of papers you need to file? Can I help you with that?'"

He did not stop there. He also stayed later than his established hours, trying to determine why people called and came in. He researched the network of who was who. He would figure out why one person stopped by the office three times in a given week, what kinds of materials they needed, and for what reason. He jotted down people's names, hoping to see how he could help them without stepping on anyone else's toes.

"I embedded myself," Lamberg says. At his first full-time position, Lamberg was always the first person at the office—sometimes waiting outside the front door until someone with more seniority (and a set of keys) showed up to unlock it. He was also the last one to leave. He set himself apart from the peers who could not wait to finish their shift. In fact, he made himself so indispensable that the executives gave him his own set of keys.

Entrepreneurial Insight

In order to create a path for growth, make yourself indispensible in whatever industry you want to be in.

It's the Client, Stupid

Even if you had unlimited business development funds, your results would be compromised if you were not client-centric. This was obvious to Jeff Hoffman, cofounder of the company that ultimately became Priceline.com. A serial entrepreneur, Hoffman has launched a string of successful companies, and his strategy for success—especially against bigger, more established competitors—does not cost a lot of money.

What enabled Hoffman to distinguish his company among the other players? "It's our deep connection with our customers," he explains. In Hoffman's world, when it comes to business development, it's all about the customer. In fact, Hoffman sees one of his most important roles as enabling his staff to serve the customer. "I'd ask clients, 'Can I send a programmer in to shadow you and see what you care about?' They'd say, 'That's kind of strange—but okay.'"

Such exposure to clients helps Hoffman and his team better serve them. It's market research at its most meaningful. Hoffman started beating out his competitors simply because his team completely understood their customers' needs. "It's all about the customer," Hoffman says. "No matter how small you are, quit guessing and go ask your clients what they care about."

While this tactic doesn't cost a lot of money, you do need to be able to free up your employees' workload so that they have the time to fully devote themselves to the client on the day set aside for shadowing. You must also train employees to be keenly observant, and—like any politician eager to win an upcoming election—they must always be deeply attuned to listening.

Entrepreneurial Insight

Understand the needs of your clients so that you can better serve them and as a result earn their loyalty.

A Couple of Dollars, Well Spent

You want to fill your team with talent? Then let them know just how much you want them around, and keep an open mind when recruiting. I discovered how important these factors were when looking to bring on a highly regarded sales professional. An accountant with whom I had conducted business recommended this person to me. At the time, he was working as a sales rep for a hair care products company, and he also worked as a maître d' to pick up some extra cash. My accountant friend was impressed with his people skills and industriousness, and the more I learned about this man, the more eager I became to make him an offer—assuming, of course, that our meeting went well. Thinking about how to make an impact so he'd join the team, I printed up a fake business card with his name on it. Our meeting went so well that, as it was ending, I handed one to him. Okay, so I misspelled his tough-to-spell last name, but I still managed to win him over. And it was perhaps the best couple of dollars I'd spent on the business.

The People in Your Corner

I have always tried to meet people who were at least a notch above my business acumen. No matter where you are in your career progression, there will always be gaps in your capabilities. It also helps to have a person of high caliber in your corner to validate your qualifications so that others are comfortable putting their faith in you.

This proved especially true when I first started Advantage Payroll and found that I really needed a strong operations person. I tried to get the individual with whom I had worked at my previous employer, but that took some convincing, which didn't come as a surprise. After all, why would someone who had a job that offered stability jump ship to join a fledgling entity? It took the endorsement of a third party, a CPA, who knew her employer as well as my business, to persuade this person to join my company. Maintaining relationships with quality people does not cost a whole lot of money, but it can help you realize immeasurable positive results.

Entrepreneurial Insight

CPAs and other centers of influence make great ambassadors for your brand.

Listening Is Free

Project Runway contestant Ari Fish knows that while good communication is the name of the game, active listening is the most important part of the equation. "You have to know how to communicate with people," she notes, adding that connecting with clients to understand their goals is the only way to expect to truly deliver and exceed expectations.

"I always try to truly listen to people when they talk, look them in the eyes, ask them questions about themselves, let them truly express themselves," she notes. "It seems like a small tip, but believe me—it really works. Meet people, travel, remember people's names, remember and recall anything you have read, and pay very close attention, because it will help you in whatever you want to do. I guarantee it."

If you don't, Fish cautions, the results can be disastrous. "If I were to tell you to make fliers and a website, and you did this but had no idea how to engage people, you would be through even before you started," she asserts. As Fish points out, effective listening is active listening, not just hearing.

> **Entrepreneurial Insight**
>
> Train your employees to become good listeners.

Third-Party Endorsements

You may offer the best widget in the world, at the best price and with the best value, but if no one knows about you, your chances at growth— or even at turning a profit—are slim. That is why a good public relations campaign is so valuable. That is the strategy Steve Davies tends to favor.

As former head of US Computer Group, Davies retained a public relations agency that helped him persuade reporters to write about his company and its rapid growth rate. He also entered all sorts of awards programs, helping the firm acquire accolades that were then written up in the press.

"It built a buzz," Davies points out. "We were a happening company. When you're growing that fast, it feels great—and everyone wants to be a part of it. We'd celebrate the wins and develop a real camaraderie. We started to become an attractive place to work; people from Grumman or Digital Equipment Corp would beat a path to our door to work here."

> **Entrepreneurial Insight**
>
> Celebrate wins in a big way. You will attract the best talent to your firm.

Of course, retaining a public relations specialist requires money, and that can add up, month after month, year after year. Still, it's one of the most effective ways to promote a business, and is much less costly than advertising in most situations. Some folks, however, do not yet have the budget to support an outside public relations firm. But lack of funds doesn't mean you shouldn't try to build buzz. Just ask South African wine importer Heritage Link Brands CEO Selena Cuffe.

"I personally pitched editors and writers," Cuffe explains, adding that these tactics had a more significant impact than they might have if she had retained the services of a public relations agency. That makes sense, given that Cuffe feels so strongly and speaks from the heart about her company's mission to spread the good news about the wines and vintners of South Africa. The media took note, with big-name publishers such as *Time* and *Inc.* magazines wanting to tell her story. "That helped tremendously in terms of awareness in the marketplace," she says.

What if your product is not quite as glamorous as wine from a faraway place, and your mission is not as noble as trying to enrich disadvantaged people who live in that place? It's worth the trouble to tell your story anyway. Reporters have to file stories, and they are always looking for an edge. Consider all of the challenges you've overcome and how you succeeded; then go ahead and pitch the reporters and editors who cover your industry. You never know who might be interested in hearing what you have to say.

Entrepreneurial Insight

Tell your success stories to the media. Public relations can go a long way toward building buzz in the right circles.

Think Big, Act Small

You could spend a lot of money on market researchers and strategists for reports on best industry trends and tactics to grow your company. Who knows; maybe it would be money well spent. However, Mike Ireland, co-owner of Martin Viette Nurseries on Long Island's north shore, learned more than he probably ever could from a third party by conducting his own research firsthand.

A second-generation principal of the company, Ireland wanted to breathe new life into the business and stand apart from the competition. "It wasn't that long ago when all plants would be rowed out," Ireland explains, adding that the practice was standard from nursery to nursery. But Ireland wanted to create a destination site, not only to draw in customers, but also to inspire them about the possibility of bringing beautiful plants into their own homes. So he learned all that he could about high-end visual merchandising.

Entrepreneurial Insight

Observe what other industries are doing well, and adopt those strategies to your own firm.

"We would go into Manhattan and visit luxury vendors like Bloomingdales and Bergdorf Goodman to see how they visually merchandise and apply the same tactics here," Ireland explains. But Ireland and his staff didn't stop there. They also took walking tours of Manhattan to internalize everything they could about how the many compelling retail stores lured in foot traffic. Soon enough, Martin Viette was creating vignettes that customers could replicate in their homes. Initially, Ireland says, the focus was on creative displays, which took the eyes off the prize: the customer. Ireland knew there was no point in creating beauty within the shop if service slipped. Therefore, the company ultimately paired the visual displays with a behind-the-scenes team to ensure that the product was labeled properly so that the salespeople could devote themselves entirely to serving customers. By sharing their goals and standards with employees, the company was able to grow sales by 20 percent.

"Competitors said we wouldn't sell anything," Ireland recalls, noting that few nurseries nowadays row out plants but instead strive to infuse imagination and creativity in their merchandising. "But instead, we've changed the way it's done. We were one of the first. We always had to think big and act small."

Even with the best innovations, as Ireland indicated to me, you must never lose focus on the customer. This is something I realized when I ran a launch party for Cossential, my start-up that matched companies seeking services with prequalified vendors at a better price than they could find independently. The company did not take off, largely because I did not do the proper research. As I explained earlier in this book, I made the major mistake of failing to realize that I was stepping on people's toes—angering the very client base I was trying to serve. You might think you are doing everything right, but if you and your team leave the customer out of the equation, the results can—and will—suffer.

Entrepreneurial Insight

Never take your eyes off your most important asset: your customer.

Why Visionaries Need Partners

It is tough to launch a firm, especially when there are budgetary constraints. It is even tougher when you are light-years ahead of the market and prospective stakeholders have yet to see the relevance of your vision.

These were the challenges that theater producer Joe Corcoran and his business partner Darren Sussman confronted when they started TheaterMania. The year was 1999, and Corcoran and Sussman, a music industry professional with online marketing experience, were looking for ways to use the Internet in selling tickets for and marketing shows. Although the Internet was growing rapidly, especially in the music industry, the theater business was not yet up to speed when it came to this kind of technology. The partners saw their niche, as Corcoran explains. At the time, most people turned to the *New York Times* to get information on shows. Yet it was expensive to list there, and lots of shows lacked the budget to advertise. As a result, many shows slipped beneath the radar. "People didn't realize there were not 40, but 400 shows," Corcoran points out. What's more, anyone who managed to discover one of the lesser-known shows would typically call the box office, leave a message, and most likely not receive a call back or confirmation.

The partners solicited investments and offered to help venues promote their shows on the Internet. Corcoran and Sussman began offering theater content to AOL, Yahoo!, and affiliate sites of network television, driving traffic to their sites and building communities, and making their pledge much more enticing at a time when the industry did not frequently utilize technology. They used these sites to offer special theater ticket promotions. "We went from zero to 40 percent of tickets sold online," he says. "We knew this was the wave of the future."

"What TheaterMania did was create a ticket option for these small shows," Corcoran adds, noting that they offered small theaters a system that gave theatergoers the ability to visit the show's website and buy tickets directly online. "We serviced 300 or so small venues that couldn't afford to do ticketing because they couldn't afford to staff a box office," says Corcoran, now chairman of the company.

It pays to have vision, but also to understand how to apply grassroots strategies to win over meaningful partners. In addition to providing editorial content and a ticketing engine, TheaterMania also allows users to check availability and charge remotely, and now it serves 800 venues.

TheaterMania's upward trajectory demonstrates why—and how—strategic partnerships can work so incredibly well. When a company is in growth mode, it often pays to collaborate with another firm that provides complementary (though not competitive) products. I have found that to be the case with my company, Advantage Payroll. Many insurance brokerage firms want to partner with my firm because my two big public competitors also sell insurance and could literally lure clients away. Insurance brokers know that I pose no such threat when they collaborate with me; and they would clearly rather have me process their clients' payrolls because they know I will not try to sell insurance to them. At the same time, these insurance brokers further their relationships with their clients by connecting them to a vetted service provider. This is something you should try to do in your own business, as it's a highly effective method of client preservation.

Entrepreneurial Insight

Team up with partners who have everything to gain by working with you.

We tend to be at our most resourceful when it seems we have no other options and our budgets are so slim we can't throw money at our challenges. Yet it is important to keep that grassroots spirit alive as we become increasingly profitable. It can make the difference in entering—and even creating—new markets, thereby allowing for sustainable growth. Yet whether you are in start-up mode or are a more established organization, there will always be a bigger entity against which you'll be forced to compete. Therefore, you will always have to be on top of your game. That is something we look at next in Chapter 7.

Summary

You must put your company in bootstrapping mode when you're first starting out in business. Consider this a survival approach; spend only on the absolute essentials, and try to use grassroots strategies wherever possible. As you look for inexpensive ways to move forward, keep the following in mind:

- Skip the fancy office space. Instead, meet clients at their office or at a restaurant. A meal out is a lot cheaper than paying expensive rent.
- Devote the time to stay on top of your trade so that your clients see you as an expert in the field.
- Diversify your customers so that you maintain a steady client base.
- Make yourself indispensible to influencers by earning their trust as you work your way up.
- Find out what your customers care about in order to best serve their needs.
- Maintain relationships with key people. You never know when you might need them on board.

- Become a good, active listener so that you can understand your clients' goals.
- Generate good public relations so that influencers are up to date with your very latest news.
- See what the big guns are doing across all industries and adopt their best strategies as your own.
- Never lose focus on the customer.
- Partner where possible with solid players.

7

Diving without a Shark Cage

WHERE I LIVE on Long Island, there are coffee shops in almost every town. These coffee shops—the good ones anyway—feature great food, tons of variety on their menu, and servers who seem genuinely interested in how your day is going as they pour more coffee and ask how you would like your eggs.

But consider this: Coffee shops are typically family-run, and the owners take care in delivering a good product despite the fact that they are swimming with the sharks. So while these entrepreneurs are providing excellent customer service, they are also competing with the eateries on either side and across the street. Surrounded by Dunkin' Donuts, McDonald's, Starbucks—what's an independent coffee shop owner to do? If ever there were a David versus Goliath scenario, this is it.

Therefore, these smaller shops need to deliver in ways that the giants cannot. Maybe they do this by creating a warm, personal environment featuring works of local artists that put the sterile décor at the big-box restaurants to shame. Maybe they remember which patrons like to order what and serve it up with a smile. Small players look for what the big—and often lethargic—guys aren't doing, and they do it better.

Entrepreneurial Insight

As a small player, you have to be on top of your game to contend with the big guns.

No matter the industry, entrepreneurs grapple with the pressures of growing their business while remaining in the big boys' shadow. This is true for almost any business owner, whether the competition stems from a national chain, a global competitor, or both.

The companies who hold their own always figure out a way to ride on the big guys' success. They know that the chains and box stores have spent money on research and market development, and those things help drive demand for a product or service. Consider again the coffee industry. The next time you see a Starbucks, see if you can't also find another coffee shop close by. Plenty of folks have figured out how to move in on Starbucks's territory, whether by providing a more personalized atmosphere, better prices, or a more varied menu. These entrepreneurs have honed in on exactly how to carve out for themselves a leading edge, not a bleeding edge.

As my business coach, Peter Cracovaner, has told me, big companies are frequently guilty of providing expensive products yet terrible customer service. This provides the opportunity for the small player to come in with boutique principles and find a spot in the marketplace. Do well what big companies do poorly, and find your niche in the marketplace. As Peter has instructed me, "Create your own foothold." Discern how and where a more powerful organization is weak, and build your company around that.

Those who persevere are the ones who stay true to the qualities that made them successful in the first place. Also, they tend to keep in mind that they can never be all things to all people. So they might as well focus on their strengths.

Consider Martin Viette Nurseries' co-owner Mike Ireland, who advises, "Even in the down times, stick with your image and your high quality, high service." I could not agree more.

This chapter examines how, in select parameters, a small firm can beat the giants at their own game.

Beware the Knee-Jerk Reaction

I started as a small provider and grew to be one of the largest independent payroll services in the New York region. Yet I'm still competing with the big, publicly owned players, which means that I always have to be on top of my game.

Entrepreneurial Insight

Sometimes the best way to compete is to sit back and watch your rivals try something new.

One of the strategies I find most effective is to set Google Alerts not only on my industry but also on my competitors. This allows me to begin every workday morning by understanding the latest and most relevant news. I want to know what is going on in my industry before my clients know, and I must be more informed than anyone else about my product and service. At the same time, I am careful not to respond with knee-jerk reactions, since sometimes, a new product from a competitor actually fails miserably. For that reason, there are times when it's best to simply take a deep breath and watch—times when doing nothing can be the best decision. After all, keeping up with the big guys can cost too much money. Still, you want to keep a watchful eye on how to best compete against them.

At my company we ask clients who have left competitors to tell us about their experiences with rival firms. We want to know what they liked and what they did not like, and we even change our service model depending on their responses. For example, we learned through our research that some customers like the reminder service that other companies provide, and we have since instituted that for all of our clients. This kind of simple, effective research can go a long way toward providing great customer service and, as a result, client retention.

Entrepreneurial Insight

One of the best and least expensive forms of market research is simply to ask new clients what they liked and did not like about their previous vendor.

Learning from the Big Boys

The formidable players do more than squeeze the hardworking independent entrepreneurs. Without intending to, they provide us with valuable lessons. So take a look. What are their deep pockets and high-powered executives doing so effectively for their companies that we can't apply to our own? Mike Ireland used that approach, studying large retailers and applying what they've done right to his own business.

"We looked at how the big boys were managing their inventory," Ireland says. As it turned out, the larger stores scanned bar codes at the cash register, something that the nursery industry hadn't yet implemented in a big way. Ireland made sure his company was one of the first garden centers to get on board with this method. "It helped us become much faster at checkout," he says.

When Home Depot and Lowe's came to town, Ireland obviously was not very happy to see them. Neither were the other independent garden centers. "A lot of garden centers panicked and lowered their prices," Ireland said, which in turn prompted owners to resort to lower quality plants and to deliver inferior service. What's more, many shop owners began selling items at cost, because they assumed that's what they needed to do to draw in foot traffic.

Entrepreneurial Insight

Dropping your prices when the big-box stores encroach can be the worst strategy of all.

"You're tempted to lower prices, and while you may get the short-term hit, you're destroying what you spent 30 years building," Ireland points out. "You wind up delivering horrible service. And the customer isn't fooled; they know a bad situation when they see one." Ireland continues, "We never took that route. We changed our model a little bit." This alternation included running a few more sales, which helped Martin Viette attract customers and rid themselves of excess inventory.

But Ireland is quick to point out that these sales didn't come because "our competitors were eating our lunch." A business owner who takes pride in the relationship his company has with customers, Ireland took note of stock on Monday, and by Thursday sent out e-mail blasts announcing what would be on sale. Throughout, Ireland and his team focused on their strengths, which, according to Ireland, are "service and quality." As he explains, "You won't find someone at the big-box stores who can talk you through a project or do it for you. That's our niche. The big boys run a very good business. We're trying to run ours differently."

Differentiators like these can set your company apart. For example, we at Advantage Payroll know that one of our big competitors gives away, each year, a $500 rebate to entice prospects to switch to their service. We keep our cool and turn that rebate against the rival firm while still maintaining our pricing. We'll pitch a client of theirs who is unaware of that deal and point out that, although our competitor's new customers receive this rebate, the loyal customer is actually paying 30 percent more than our rate. That is never happy news for the client, and it erodes our competition's client base. Like Ireland, we stick to our guns by offering the right product and service at the right price. We sell the value of our service to our entire client base, which has increased our close rate substantially because our competitor's clients realized that they were getting a raw deal.

Entrepreneurial Insight

Customer service can be the real differentiator between you and your biggest competitor.

Use Your Smarts

Entrepreneurs typically are very resourceful. Their quick thinking, combined with what is often a palpable enthusiasm, can help them spot the kinds of opportunities that make the difference in getting their business off the ground. It also helps a company stay true to its mission and create a distinct and sustainable brand. Consider Heritage Link Brands' CEO Selena Cuffe, who runs her company according to a mission that aims to help lift South Africa's black population out of poverty. As she points out, very few wineries in South Africa have black owners. She says. "Eighty-five percent of the population there is black. No one else connected the dots on that. For me, it's incredibly important to help move along the transformation to a more equitable country."

The market responds to Cuffe's enthusiasm, which can go a long way. Recently, when I gave a presentation to an audience of 500 at a regional organization called "Keep It On Long Island," I received more than 50 e-mails from attendees who said they liked my enthusiasm for local businesses. It is a subject close to my heart, and people responded to that sincerity.

Entrepreneurial Insight

One of your best assets can be the enthusiasm you bring to the market.

Find the Other Guys' Weak Spots

Tell me what the big guys do poorly.
—Jeff Hoffman, cofounder and CEO in the
Priceline.com family of companies

Okay, so maybe an independent retailer should not expect to take down Macy's, at least not anytime soon. But when it comes to wooing and retaining customers, the smaller guys can figure out what the chain is doing wrong, and then make a point of doing the opposite. That is the philosophy by which Jeff Hoffman lives and works.

"Tell me what the big guys do poorly," Hoffman says. Once he knows, he shapes his dialogue to show a prospect that he can deliver what the competitor has not. That is how he gets his foot in the door; and once he's there, he has his priorities straight. "The only thing that matters is the paying customer," he says.

Of course, once you have won over a series of clients, you run the risk of growing to the point where you might lose the all-important ability to act nimbly. That is where leadership plays a big role. "You need to make an intentional effort," Hoffman advises. "You have to constantly light a fire behind your team. Don't let them drift into complacency, or you'll start thinking you're right, and you'll risk losing that relentless drive that made you so successful in the first place."

So don't get too comfortable, Hoffman warns. "Finish strong. Remember how you got to this point."

Innovators Rule

Business has always been tough. But those who understand how to put technology to work for them—and I mean *really work* for them—can blow the big boys out of the water. These sleeping giants will never know what hit them.

> ### Entrepreneurial Insight
>
> Put technology—the true equalizer—to work for you in order to compete effectively in the marketplace, even against your largest rivals.

Joe Corcoran certainly put technology to work for him when he cofounded TheaterMania. Up until that point, the typically strapped-for-cash theater productions had difficulty getting the word out about their shows.

But the Internet offered something more, namely reports that show the client how an ad campaign performs. "As we know, the beauty of the Internet—as opposed to billboards and *New York Times* ads—is that you can track your efforts and their results," Corcoran says. "It's a breakthrough for marketers. They can either shift gears, or continue to invest in areas where they see success."

TheaterMania also provided the ability to offer content, which prompts Internet users to read the latest news about the theater and see what shows are playing. The platform drives traffic to the theater's website rather than to Ticketmaster, and allows visitors to learn more about the show and order tickets. The Internet experience is designed to make theatergoers feel like they are buying tickets from the show's box office rather than through TheaterMania.

And while TheaterMania has largely become a household name—at least in the New York region—the company is making a point of staying nimble, especially in the current economic climate. They offer theaters the option to "give us a straight commission on every ticket sold, or pay us a flat fee," Corcoran says. "It gives presenters lots of options about the best way to sell a theater ticket. You have to be creative these days."

> ### Entrepreneurial Insight
>
> Once you get a foothold in the market, remember to stay nimble so that you can jump in different directions as needed.

Don't Be Afraid to Be Small

Remaining small is just fine for Broadway and off-Broadway producer Ken Davenport. In a landscape dotted with the likes of Andrew Lloyd Webber and other heavy hitters, Davenport finds that being small is actually a strength. "I compete by remaining small," Davenport explains. "I can execute faster. I don't have huge overhead. If I have an idea, I can get it done tomorrow; there is no bureaucracy and nobody to answer to."

Davenport is happy to work on a small scale. He finds the larger organizations more unwieldy, and he prefers being hands-on. Some owners prefer to pass off the business responsibilities to others and go play golf. There's nothing wrong with either approach. You just need to make the right decision for you.

A Double Isn't Bad, but a Home Run Is Better

You're only as good as your last win, especially if you are a small business. So stay focused on winning every time. That's an approach that is working nicely for David Becker, president of Philippe Becker, the San Francisco branding and packaging agency that counts Whole Foods, Safeway, and many other big names as clients.

"I believe we're as good as it gets," Becker states. "We're at the top of our game, and we can play with anyone. Now we have the track record to prove it."

Being a small fish in a pond where the fish are enormous seems to work out nicely for Becker. "Our size allows us to be more creative, more nimble, and pay more attention to the client. We're at a sweet spot between the mom-and-pops and the multinational firms. When you're competing with the big guys, it's ultimately the quality of the product that makes a difference. If you can deliver home run after home run, people take note. The more we go along, the more wins we have, and the more out phone calls get returned."

Slow, Steady, and Without Temptation

Scott Snibbe, of Snibbe Interactive, takes the slow-and-steady approach to growth. While he knows that the bigger players may have more money, experience has taught him that a big influx of outside investment cash can kill a business.

"I learned more from mistakes," Snibbe says, speaking about a company he'd owned that went out of business. "We were funded by venture capitalists. We had two great guys who would come in every month for a board meeting and give quick advice." But that advice was not well founded, and the company ultimately could not sustain itself. "After we went out of business, I realized I could have continued to build it if I had grown it in a different way. They poured millions of dollars in, and it failed quickly."

Slow and steady is now the mantra with Snibbe's current business, and he rejected any enticements to entertain venture capital this time around. "When I started, we had no venture capital. We were always starved for cash," he says. "But we pay our way. We respond to customers. We develop slowly and steadily, rather than fast out the market. That kind of growth is not sustainable. If you are spending a couple million dollars, you need revenue fast."

This slow-and-steady approach seems to be working out nicely for Snibbe. "We're in the $1 million to $5 million range," Snibbe says. "In the first three years, we almost tripled our revenues year over year. Last year, 2009, was a rough year for everyone, but our approach paid off." Several competitors shut down. One of them, Snibbe notes, had $120 million from investors. As Snibbe points out, money, seductive as it is, cannot necessarily buy sustainability.

Since I did not have money when I started my business, I found a partner who did, rather than use venture capital. Still, I could not have started my business without that financial assistance. Yet it's key to find investors who become an integral part of getting you where you want to go. I have been able to maintain control in meeting my goals, and that has paid off, even in a bad economy. In 2009, for instance, my company was up 5 percent during a severe recession in which most people were down 10 to 15 percent. In 2010, we were up 16 percent. Those results are a testament to controlled growth—not overspending—and building a sustainable brand. It doesn't mean that raising cash to grow fast can be a bad thing; I simply chose not to conduct my company this way. Otherwise, I would have given up control of my firm. Certainly, it is better to be a 100 percent owner than a 10 percent owner—that is, if you want to control your own destiny. Once you take someone's money, you lose a lot of this control.

Entrepreneurial Insight

Venture capital money, if you can get it, may look tempting—but you could wind up losing control of your company.

Giants? What Giants?

Steve Davies, former head of US Computer Group, never minded the giants. Sure, he was competing with powerful names like Northrop Grumman and Bell Atlantic, but that didn't seem to bother him in the least.

"Basically there were five nationwide players, and we were a regional player," he explains. So Davies played the local card, flaunting his company as the provider that cared about their clients' experience. "Our competition was very poor, administratively," he says. He began to see that clients and prospects cared about what was in the contract, information that they could not always readily obtain. "We were very organized in this area; providing information to clients was very important to us." Davies found that granting clients the access and service they needed was critical. "You give it to them however you can; if they're happy, that's ultimately really all that matters."

Even the Best Ideas Need Help

As an entrepreneur, I have what seems like thousands of distinct thoughts in my head each day. Sifting through them and accessing what I need to know can be a challenge. When I focus, I have to hyper-focus, which is often difficult, considering that I probably have attention deficit/hyperactivity disorder (though in all fairness, I have never been diagnosed). To help counter this tendency to drift mentally, I surround myself with key people who have the skills that I lack and can help me complete a job better than I ever could on my own.

One of those key people I placed in my circle is a business coach. If you can afford to retain one, it may be the best money you ever spent. Entrepreneurs and businesses are pulled in so many directions, and you cannot possibly know everything. I am not normally a fan of hiring consultants, but there is no question that my coach has helped me run my business better.

Entrepreneurial Insight

Even the best ideas require help, so be sure to get the best support available, whether from a coach or a mentor.

I am a big believer in the importance of ideas and the ability to implement them in order to achieve success on both a professional and personal level. However, these ideas must be executed well. So, start this exercise with an image, a deep-seated notion, such as Henry Ford's vision of a motorcar that everyone could afford to drive. Remember, at that time only the very wealthy could afford cars. Next, consider what you need to put in place in order for that vision to become a reality. Ford, for example, came up with the assembly line and decided to make the cars all black as the least expensive route to achieving his vision. In addition, Ford made sure that assembly line workers would make enough money so that they could afford the cars, which would then be visible on the street and help to drive demand for the product. Finally, complete the vision by determining the physical manifestation and result. In Ford's example, the result is the actual car.

The space between the ideas and concepts and the physical manifestation is your blueprint, a component that my coach Peter says is lacking in most business plans. So when building your idea, ask yourself about the blueprint; or, as Peter puts it, "Every action step needs a period of incubation to allow the idea to become a physical reality." Once you understand your place in the market and you map out your blueprint to execute your idea, you will improve your odds against the big contenders. Still, you will never eliminate the risks, a topic we delve into more deeply in Chapter 8.

> *Every action step needs a period of incubation to allow the idea to become a physical reality.*
> —Peter Cracovaner, Basso On Business coach

Summary

It can seem like really bad news when a big-box competitor encroaches on your game. But the worst thing you can do is panic. Remember, plenty of entrepreneurs launch their companies and realize tremendous success in spite of the big guns, and you can too. Here are some tips to help you stay on the leading edge:

- Look for ways in which big business is weak, and build your company around that.
- Set Google Alerts for your industry and competitors in order to find out what is going on in the marketplace in real time, and if need be, respond accordingly.
- Borrow strategies from the big players to help you improve your game.
- Don't drop your prices in response to the large competitors. You will likely wind up with subpar goods and services.
- When a rival offers deals for new customers, point out to your own market share that you offer good, consistent pricing to all of your clients, all year round.
- Remember, sincere enthusiasm is usually well received.
- Keep your focus on the paying customer, the one who matters most.
- Stay nimble, even as you grow.
- Deploy technology to jump-start innovation and create your own foothold in the market.

- Stay on top of your game. Hit home run after home run, and the market will take note.
- Think twice before accepting venture capital money so that you can maintain control of your organization's destiny.
- Remember that the giants often get sloppy and fail to realize when their customers become unhappy. This scenario often provides ample opportunity for smaller and more nimble players to move in on the giants' territory.
- You should have a blueprint that specifies a systematic action plan for carrying out your vision and seeing results.

8

Fun with Risks

YOU DO NOT have to be a daredevil to make it in business. However, you'll likely be pressed to step out of your comfort zone in order to truly make a go of your venture at some point. That can mean kissing your steady nine-to-five job goodbye and devoting yourself full time to your start-up, or putting your money where your mouth is to fund your endeavor. It might require that you put yourself on the line to win the faith of creditors, investors, and other stakeholders. Sure, it is the kind of adrenaline rush that can get your heart racing, but it doesn't mean you have to lose your shirt. That all-or-nothing situation is probably one where the odds are against you, unless you literally have nothing to lose. While I am all for taking risks, I truly believe that they have to be smart risks.

Entrepreneurial Insight

Most success requires a certain amount of risk, but that doesn't mean you have to lose your shirt.

Consider the outlook of skydiving enthusiast and San Francisco–based branding and packaging entrepreneur David Becker. "As a skydiver, you focus on what you have control over—your training, your judgment about when to go or not, the equipment you choose," Becker explains. The same outlook applies to business: Stay measured, be prepared, and understand how much you can afford to lose before you take the plunge.

You will never know the heights you can reach without some amount of risk. But it *is* possible to enjoy yourself in the process. This chapter looks at how you can have fun in business without losing your shirt.

Vegas, Here We Come

As a 20-something, I had very little to lose—no family to support, no mortgage to pay. So taking risks, such as investing in a business, was not as scary as it might have been later in life. I'm now in my thirties, and I haven't given up taking risks; in fact, quite the opposite. But nowadays, I'll only take calculated risks. It's like going to Las Vegas knowing exactly how much you're willing to lose, and no more. Just as a group of friends might plan an annual trip to Vegas for some fun, I set out on a new venture every year with some cash that I have set aside to invest. That's how I allowed myself the leeway to become a founder of a community bank, a Broadway investor, and join other enterprises. Recognizing that I might not see any return, I also knew that I could win big—*really* big.

The chance to win big is very appealing. It has led me to other endeavors, such as investing in a horror film, *T.N.T.*, in which a killer murders victims by blowing people up. I trusted the team behind it, and there is a chance that this production may go from DVD to theaters. Sure, there is a better than 90 percent chance that I will lose my investment, but I can afford to do it. I'm not losing my mortgage payment or jeopardizing my kids' college education. So as far as I'm concerned, the risk is worth taking.

Entrepreneurial Insight

Take risks that allow you to maintain a comfortable level of control. Smart risk-taking requires all kinds of calculations and assessments, so do your homework. Plan for the best outcomes, but understand that you may not always meet your goals.

Yet while owning a successful company affords me the opportunity to take chances, perhaps the biggest risk I have ever taken is the one I am currently pursuing. Right now, I am investing my time and energy at what may be the peak of my career, as well as of my physical and mental acuity, as I push forward with Basso On Business and develop a brand that inspires the entrepreneurial spirit. There is a huge risk in that, since I'm hoping and working hard while not knowing if it will pan out. Yet as someone who has invested in entertainment, I recognize that I like it so much that I am now making the entertainment *me*. Somehow, that seems to me to be less of a wild card.

It allows me as the investor a lot more control, at least when it comes to developing the product.

So, while there is risk, it is calculated—one that, with the proper planning and training, I hope will work. Business is not much different. You need to plan for the best outcome but realize that without taking some kind of risk, you will probably not reach your goal.

Analyze Your Bets Before You Gamble

Unlike David Becker, most of us are not skydivers. Still, we probably could learn a thing or two from the parallels he draws between skydiving and business. After all, both potentially could prove hazardous, unless you take steps to mitigate the exposure. As Becker puts it, "Risks aren't often accurately perceived. Human beings are pretty poor judges of risk in that they're not rational about it. They're not good at assessing risk; for example, they're perfectly happy to text and drive at the same time."

Becker adds that by not accurately assessing risks, people fail to recognize what they can do to manage them. "It's like driving. Some people drive for 40 years and nothing happens, and some get into accidents all the time. Lots of people mountain-climb and push the envelope and get into trouble. Some can't even imagine that there's leeway."

This, according to Becker, is why it is so important to understand the parameters, whether you are skydiving or thinking about investing your hard-earned cash into a commercial venture. "It's the same in business. You're making bets, but you can manage them with good analysis and judgment," Becker notes. "Both scenarios require that you try to disassociate your emotions from the rational. Not that I would say skydiving is rational, but it's rational that we're emotional human beings who want to do things to connect with the universe. When you're flying, you're doing something so much bigger than you; so your problems don't seem that big. A day of skydiving is like taking a mental three-day vacation—which some people do via meditation."

While meditation is arguably the safer route, skydiving seems to fuel Becker's creativity, an especially critical quality in the design business. And risk and creativity go hand in hand. It is this combination that Becker brings to his clients, helping him grow his business.

Sometimes we take risks for granted in our daily lives, and Becker is acutely aware of this fact. "I live in San Francisco," he notes. "I could die in an earthquake. That's the reality. We're not going to live forever. There's stuff you can do about it, and stuff you can't. You have parameters. Unless you want to live a hundred feet underground in a bunker—that's not living."

So take the risks and soar to new heights, but also borrow some analogies from Becker. Get the best equipment possible, check the weather, and exercise good judgment. Emotion and vulnerability are never a good mix.

Risks from the Very First Step

The simple act of hanging out your shingle signifies entrepreneurial risk. The sign itself announces to the world that you are open for business. But to the entrepreneur posting the sign, it means so much more.

It means, "Yes, I did it. I took the risk."

That can be especially true for those who leave a comfortable job. Just ask Heritage Link Brands CEO Selena Cuffe. "If giving up the security of a well-paying job to import wines from South Africa isn't risky, I'm not sure what is," she says. Yet Cuffe felt she had been preparing for this moment even while sitting through seemingly lofty lectures at Harvard Business School. "I've had incredible teachers," she notes. "They mentored me to believe anything was possible. With the case method of learning in a protagonist's shoes, you are the entrepreneur and decision maker. In class, I could use these examples to test out my decisions on how to manage certain issues and mitigate risk, depending on the situation. And they were pretty good decisions."

That academic preparation, and her later stints in the corporate and nonprofit world, emboldened Cuffe to open her business, no matter how difficult the odds might have appeared to someone else. But Cuffe sounds downright calculating and determined to come out a winner. "I'm a wine importer in the business of brand building," she notes. "The average person would have walked away.

Getting into this business require us to make decisions based on qualitative research on what customers wanted, rather than our opinion. We also started going to school to step up our game in the wine business."

That's not to say the endeavor didn't come with its own set of pressures for Cuffe, who had quit her job and also just had a baby. "The personal risk added stress," she acknowledges. "But it brought credibility to what we were doing. We were serious about it. And that helped people's perceptions of the business."

Is that the route everyone should take? Perhaps not. But life is filled with seize-the-moment kinds of opportunities, both professionally and personally. "We decided to have two children in a five-year period—three, if you count the business," Cuffe says with a laugh. "Looking back, it was idealistic, optimistic, and a little crazy."

Convincing Others to Come Along for the Ride

As a Broadway and off-Broadway producer, Ken Davenport takes a gamble. He has sharpened his instinct to know what kind of show is a good bet. Still, bet is the operative word. Numerous factors contribute to a show's eventual success or failure—some in his control and some out of it. It is a risky endeavor for sure, and to raise the stakes even higher, Davenport, who has had more wins than losses, gets other people to invest their money into his projects. He needs these investors; as he points out, it takes many people to put on a show. They are betting on his winning streak and hoping for another hit. And there's always the chance that they could cease to believe in him.

"It's devastating to me to lose people's money, more so for me than for the investor," Davenport states. "I worked so hard; I take it very personally. People say this is a business and know that there are risks, but I tell my investors, 'You are investing in my track record of seven for nine in an industry that is one out of five. Please look at me as someone to stick with. One day I will have my *Wicked*. It's a long-term process, and eventually we'll hit.'"

To sweeten the journey, Davenport points out, "I've never lost money when I'm the lead producer." To hedge his bets, he cuts costs, working with smaller projects that allow for more flexibility.

He is mitigating the risk for his investors and building his reputation as a result.

Entrepreneurial Insight

If you want people to take a risk with you, it helps to have a good track record.

The Smaller the Better, Sometimes

If you don't push the envelope, you don't live.
—Jeff Hoffman, cofounder and CEO in the
Priceline.com family of companies

It's ironic how an individual or a small organization can be so risk-prone, perhaps perilously so, while some of the bigger outfits, who can afford to take a hit, are reluctant to try something new. As Jeff Hoffman puts it, many larger companies are "averse to making change." Yet smaller organizations often are flexible enough to right the ship. "In a little company, you can shake it off," he notes.

Hoffman was not one afraid to take a risk. He built software companies, bidding on work while he didn't even know how to write software. "I'd give big-time presentations when I was not sure how it would work," he says. "Then, after winning the bid, I'd figure it out."

Hoffman would take a chance, scramble to make it work, and then enjoy the ride. It is an approach he takes in his personal life too: setting his sights on an idea, figuring it out along the way, and then taking in the adventure.

"I like to do global exploring," he says. "When the Berlin Wall came down, I went to the airport and flew to Berlin, and then realized that I didn't even know where the Berlin Wall was. I had no hotel reservation. I was up all night with the Germans during my first day there." At one point, Hoffman wound up in a cab, joking around with his taxi driver. Hoffman said to him, "Let's go to your house to eat." And lo and behold—the driver invited Hoffman to his home. "If you don't push the envelope, you don't live," Hoffman says.

> ### Entrepreneurial Insight
>
> Risk is often one of the most important ingredients needed to achieve that all-important success.

You Don't Have to Go Whitewater Rafting to Take Risks

There are deals that don't work out—don't let that jam you up.
— Evan Lamberg, music publishing executive

Music publishing executive Evan Lamberg is not much for taking physical risks, opting more for working out on a treadmill than, say, whitewater rafting. Still, he attributes much of his professional success to taking chances. In fact, you could say his entire career stemmed from taking a single, substantial risk: stepping off the path to medical school so that he could enter the music industry.

Lamberg also takes risks with artists as he gets to know them and their work. He's not afraid to green-light a project after others have claimed that a particular artist or record is not going to work. "I have a good track record that way," Lamberg reveals. "I don't agree with someone else's decision, and I'm doing it anyway. My riskiest deals have translated into some of my greatest successes."

Lamberg pointed to two of these triumphs: bands Hootie and the Blowfish and Matchbox Twenty. Lamberg was instantly drawn to Hootie and the Blowfish upon first hearing them, and he figured if the world heard their music, they'd embrace it, too. And when he heard Matchbox Twenty's Rob Thomas, Lamberg said, "I gotta bet on that songwriter."

Both bands were unknowns and unsigned. "It would have been easier to bow to pressure internally and externally," Lamberg concedes. But he took the gamble, and in both cases it worked. There was always the chance that it wouldn't—that's a given, especially in the music business. "There are deals that don't work out," Lamberg says. "But you can't let that jam you up."

Yet while Lamberg admits that an accumulation of "fails" poses problems, it's almost always worse to cave in to the fear that a deal may not succeed. That kind of fear leads to paralysis. And if you allow that to happen, you won't get anywhere.

Protect Your Risk from the Get-Go

I want no idea of mine to be so talked about that it becomes dead before its arrival.

—Ari Fish, *Project Runway* contestant

While risk can set creativity free, it is also vital to protect that creativity. *Project Runway* contestant Ari Fish is fierce about guarding her ideas, holding them close until they are ready for launch.

"I have a tendency to hide in the shadows when I work, as I did when I was little," she notes. "I keep my ideas to myself so as to truly, and ideally, give birth to them in a certain insular manner. I don't want anyone to discuss any of my ideas so much that it dies before its arrival."

I take the opposite approach. I tend to talk a great deal about a project when I start it; I feel that it makes me accountable and creates a kind of pressure to produce. For instance, I have not been quiet about writing this book, and as a result, I am constantly asked about the publication date. I use it as a tool. I do not mind sharing my ideas, because I believe even if someone did attempt to copy me or utilize my concepts, they would not do it the way I intended it to be. For example, there was one occasion when a competitor did attempt to replicate one of my programs, the Entrepreneurial Advantage Residual Network, which was an independent program for people to sell payroll services as representatives of my company. The competitor who tried to launch a similar program put no branding or marketing behind it, and it folded after two months. So I'm not afraid to share ideas; I'm confident that I'm going to do the better job.

Facing Changes

Risk usually means change, and that can sound daunting to some people. Off-Broadway producer Joe Corcoran, however, sees change as positive, even though it can also be disruptive.

"Change is good. It's healthy. You grow most from change," he points out. Corcoran notes that his family has moved back and forth from New York City to Los Angeles (along with a stint in San Francisco), all in the name of opening shows. Several years ago, they added a house in the Berkshires to the mix, where they relocated for a time before returning to New York. Then Corcoran's wife received a fellowship in a writing-for-performance program in Los Angeles, where they relocated again, even though their daughter was a senior in high school who would graduate in a few months. Then, within six months of the move, the family had to deal with an unexpected blow when Corcoran was diagnosed with lung cancer. At that time, the family returned to the Berkshires.

"My family was just starting to establish friendships," he says. "But I didn't want to mess around here. I have nurses and doctors here where I've had intensive treatment."

It was while healing—a period most would consider still vulnerable—that Corcoran's wife set up a blog where he could tell his story and people could post a message. The process "was life-changing for me," Corcoran says. "I'm thinking what I want to do for the rest of my life. It's still fresh."

Corcoran's knack for risk-taking, though, has not diminished due to this experience. Right now, he is working on a version of *Dr. Zhivago* in Australia that he plans to bring to Broadway. Between lining up the director, coordinating with investors, the theater, the worldwide rights, and more—the production has experienced its share of bruises. "It's been a struggle," Corcoran admits. "But I imagine it every day in my mind, standing ovations every night." The show has since opened to favorable reviews. Corcoran explains that he made the show smaller, and therefore less costly to produce, to meet current economic demands. "It's been a huge challenge for me for more than two years," he says.

A huge challenge, yes; but Corcoran is assessing the playing field to make sure that his production has a shot on Broadway. He is taking that risk, not afraid to navigate change to make the show work. Will it all come together? It may be too soon to say for sure. But one thing seems certain: Corcoran is looking at risk and change, and seeing personal growth and possibilities in the view. And to Corcoran, that's a very positive thing.

Entrepreneurial Insight

Risks may need some fine-tuning. But that doesn't mean you shouldn't take them.

Other People's Money

Some claim that investing with other people's money is the best way to mitigate risk. But that can come with its own set of pressures, whether the money is from investors, a bank, or some third party, as the former head of US Computer Group, Steve Davies, well knows.

"We moved to the United States from England when my kids were three and five," he says. "We bought a house, and within four months I was out of a job. That's why I bought this small maintenance company. I was partners with people in England who invested in my company. I put up 40 percent; they put up 60."

However, launching the company in this way didn't necessarily detach Davies from the risk of financial responsibility. "We were always undercapitalized," Davies recalls. "I was a minority shareholder; I was guaranteeing all the bank debt. At one point I was guaranteeing $7 million in bank debt, but I wasn't worth it."

Davies's bank ultimately told him to find another bank, and he wound up with an asset-based lender on the West Coast, which took him off the bank personal guarantee. "They controlled the receivables," Davies points out. "I would advise people against that route, but if you have to have the money, it's like heroin—completely addictive."

About That Adrenaline Rush

Not every entrepreneur seeks that adrenaline rush inherent with flying, motocross, or some other extreme sport. But when they achieve that kind of high in business, they tend to want more.

Davies puts it this way: "I worked incredibly hard, and my whole recreational life suffered. I'm not a danger seeker. But in business, it's the thrill of the kill. It's not about the money; it's the charge of success that comes when you win a piece of business. I found this to be true in better salespeople. They're not driven by commission, but by success. It's a yardstick for sure."

Entrepreneurial Insight

Successful risk-taking may be the ultimate adrenaline rush in business.

I can vouch for that philosophy. While I, of course, wanted financial success in the early years of my career, it was more appealing to score in the marketplace. Sure, that's easy to say once you achieve success. Looking back, however, it was the journey to success that was the most satisfying (though making the money clearly didn't hurt, either).

You may be hard-pressed to match the force of a determined risk-taker, unless, of course, you couple that enthusiasm with the confidence that comes with experience. We look at the importance of life lessons next in Chapter 9.

Summary

Simply being in business requires a certain amount of risk. But in order to truly soar, most entrepreneurs need to *embrace* risk. Risk should not necessarily prompt fear. With the proper assessments, you can understand how far to push the limit before it is time to change course. Here are some strategies to help you better understand and prepare yourself to take risks:

- You should take on risk understanding exactly how much you can afford to lose.
- Know that while you may not see any return, you can also win big—*really* big.

- Understand that there is leeway with risk, so determine your options from the outset.
- Risk, with all its exhilaration, can fuel creativity like nothing else can.
- Undergo some training—whether in school or, even better, through a mentor—to help you learn how to mitigate risk.
- Build a track record of wins so that investors are more comfortable betting on you.
- Stay nimble enough to take on change.
- Become comfortable with the way risk feels. It can lead to your greatest successes.
- Realize that caving in to fear can lead to more of a failure than taking a chance.
- Remember that risk can also prompt growth.
- Risk often brings with it the thrill of the kill, which can be more rewarding than any kind of cash incentive.

9

The Corporate Game

WOULD-BE ENTREPRENEURS ARE all too often itching to break free of the nine-to-five world so that they no longer have to work for "the man." Perhaps they're tired of taking orders from someone else or being a cog in the wheel, and they want to make their own decisions and run with their ideas.

My advice to these eager individuals? *Slow down*. Even if your ideas are the best in the business, there is much to be learned in the corporate world. Think of your time there as practical experience in a live lab. What's working? What isn't? What is your boss doing that is completely stupid, or that is actually worth emulating? As you bide your time in the corporate world, you will have ample opportunity to sharpen your skills, whether it's learning new systems and procedures, or playing a role, no matter how small, in how deals get done. This is the time to learn, so keep your eyes wide open.

Entrepreneurial Insight

Working in the corporate world can provide good opportunities to hone your business acumen.

While you are in your live lab, get to know the people around you, from your peers to the higher-ups, as well as clients, vendors, and service people. These are the people who may potentially be part of your professional circle years from now.

And don't think that these lessons are only available in the world of Fortune 500 companies, Silicon Valley sensations, or other highly successful ventures. There is plenty to be learned over at the corner deli shop, where you could be a fly on the wall as the owner smoothes things over with creditors, or where you might learn everything you need to know about customer service and presentation.

Of course, this strategy may be difficult to take on if, say, you despise your employer, but even in such an environment, I'd argue that there are plenty of lessons worth gleaning, probably on what *not* to do.

If you're lucky enough to work in a positive environment, your time there may later prove to be more worthwhile than sitting in any business school classroom.

As Adam Schwam, chief executive officer of Long Island IT company Sandwire, told me, working for an enterprising entrepreneur allowed him to witness someone experiencing both successes and failures. "I learned that it is never impossible to do anything." That's a powerful lesson, and again, not something you'll likely learn first-hand in a classroom, no matter how prestigious the institution.

This chapter examines the importance of picking up life lessons wherever possible as you set yourself up for something bigger than your present occupation.

Throw That Dough in the Air

Though I was never big on working for someone else, I played the game whenever I did have such a job, and I always took in everything I could. My top priority was to deliver and be the best one in the office, even if the job consisted of tasks I hated. A classic example is the stint I spent washing dishes in a busy restaurant kitchen. I got through this job because I knew it would be for just a brief moment in time. So I learned what I could about being a team player and about management, noting what I liked and disliked about people and operations while on the job.

When I worked at a pizzeria in South Jersey, I started as a dishwasher and watched the entire operation flow from my less-than-desirable (but highly enlightening) vantage point. It was quite a learning experience. I clearly saw who was in charge, who was lazy, who was a joker, and who went the extra mile. I marveled at what went well in the orchestration of a kitchen that had to be kept in good working order: the orders coming in and being processed, dishes being brought back, and starting the cycle all over again, as customers continued to pour into the restaurant. I also observed how occasional chaos—a kitchen losing its rhythm, orders screwed up—was always triggered by human emotion, such as the time the pizza maker had been in a car accident, or a server grew angry about a lousy tip. It took skill to get the staff back on track. Depending on his mood, the owner would either try to placate everyone to make it work, or he'd start screaming. It drove home a crucial point: People skills are, without a doubt, the most important skills to have in business.

I pressed the owner to let me try to run the pizza ovens, and he practically laughed me out of the place. But I did not give up. Finally, he let me become a helper, and I learned how to create a pizza, from making the sauce to throwing the dough in the air, which I did pretty well. I even filled in when the regular guy could not make it or wanted a weekend off. I had learned from the experts and made myself a valuable commodity. These are lessons to take with you as you move on in life. (The better pay is nice too.)

Entrepreneurial Insight

While working for someone else, try to work in as many job positions as possible so that you can pick up new skills and broaden your network along the way.

Not Every Big Company Is Evil

Before David Becker launched the San Francisco branding and packaging agency Philippe Becker, he worked for Intuit, the maker of business accounting software QuickBooks. He sharpened his knowledge of technology and the Web while employed in Silicon Valley during the height of the mid-1990s, the dot-com years. Then he moved on to Frog Design, Inc., a leading product design firm that has offices in San Francisco and around the world.

The corporate world taught Becker some important lessons about operating a business. "Intuit was the best-run company I ever worked for," he says. Why? "They only hire the best people." Becker suggests that it is indeed the people, and their passion for doing good work, that enable a company to soar. Diplomas and fancy degrees, by themselves, will not carry a business far at all. That is why I like to look people in the eye when I'm interacting with them professionally, whether they are working for me or I am working for them. I like to know what inspires and motivates the people in my business circle.

Entrepreneurial Insight

Pick up whatever knowledge you can about business operations while working for someone else.

As Becker points out, "Every company says that it's about the people. It tends to be the smart people who can learn and evolve." He also explains that working for a big corporate player helps would-be entrepreneurs to better understand the landscape: "I learned that not all mega-companies are bad," Becker says. "You're not working for the man if you work for a large company. And we need small companies to play in areas in which the big companies can't play."

But perhaps what Becker learned most from his time in the corporate world was the power of innovation. "The mid-1990s was a very exciting time in Silicon Valley," Becker says. "It fueled my desire to do even more exciting stuff, since something big was happening every day." Of course, when you surround yourself with a team of bright, passionate people, the potential for success increases much more.

Everyday Case Study/Leadership Roles

Subject business: East Coast Refrigeration, Inc.

Owner Name: Jeff Tempone

View Video at: www.BassoOnBusiness.com

Jeff Tempone can fix nearly anything, but his particular fascination with refrigeration started while he worked at an ice skating rink where he played hockey as a teenager. He was always curious about how the ice was made, and exactly what kept it so cold all the time. He never imagined that he would be running his own growing refrigeration business in a few years. Though his company is less than six years old and is already serving a number of large contracts, that's not satisfying enough for Jeff. He wants his business to be one of the refrigeration leaders in the entire region.

There is only one problem with Jeff's plan. Well, more than one actually. Jeff had run into some significant snags along the way, and he readily confessed that most of these issues are of his own making. Recently, my crew stopped by his location, and Jeff and I got to talking about his operation. Through the course of our conversations, we uncovered some challenges that, if left unchecked, could have made it nearly impossible for his business to continue to succeed and grow.

Jeff had fewer than 10 employees, which certainly categorizes him as a small business owner. We asked him about his staff and each player's role within his organization. He explained that he had an office manager; however, when we inquired exactly what her duties were or if she had a job description to fulfill, Jeff replied that he was actually not clear on her exact role, and that she currently had no job description. Well, how could he expect her to do a good job if she wasn't even entirely sure about what she was supposed to be doing?

Jeff also did not have a company mission statement that he could use to unite his team behind. Quite the contrary; actually, he was at the mercy of his staff, and wasn't giving them a solid reason to follow him down the path to success. Jeff and his employees did not share the same vision of what the company was, how it was going to grow, and what roles they played within the organization. Therefore, Jeff knew that he needed to make his staff feel that they could have a career with his company, not just a job. The people who worked for him considered their jobs to be a nine-to-five source of a paycheck, nothing more.

We had a conversation with one salesperson who, according to Jeff, was incapable of really selling anything. While this person had the required technical experience, he had no ability to communicate product knowledge to a prospective client. We pressed Jeff about the training process for his sales force. Jeff admitted that it was his own fault that this individual was in the wrong role. He knew that as the company's leader, he had either

(*continued*)

(*continued*)
hired the wrong person or did not train him properly to gain the sales results he so desperately wanted.

Now on to the bigger issue: Jeff also took a hard look at his own traits and tactics, and he saw some gaping holes in his own ability to guide his team. Many of these holes came as a result of his leadership and organizational style. It was not a lack of intelligence or street smarts; it was a lack of knowledge of how to manage a group of employees. In fact, Jeff's technical skill level rivaled that of any expert in his field. It's just that running a company doesn't merely require being good at one thing. Jeff needed to have a quiver full of administrative and technical arrows before he could truly lead his company.

We suggested that Jeff take a leadership course to help him gain the vital skills he needed to lead his company and rally the troops behind him. To accomplish his personal goal of making his organization a major player in the region, Jeff needed to be leading a well-trained, eager, and united workforce. He also had to focus more carefully on recruiting, training, and devising appropriate job descriptions to make policies and procedures more systematic.

Jeff did not let more than a week go by before he started making big changes. Not only did he write a company mission statement, he also made the enlightened decision to ask each of his staff members to write their own personal mission statements. He then reviewed these documents with his employees and used them to come up with a final version together. If his staff makes decisions based on a mission they've mutually created, they can't go wrong. Jeff also hired an outside consultant to write job descriptions as well as an exhaustive employee manual with detailed policies and procedures.

Jeff exudes a new sense of confidence about his business that was not present before; he is becoming the leader his company must have in order to succeed. If Jeff continues his hard work and persists in increasing his knowledge or seeking outside help when he needs it, he will become the regional leader he wants to be.

Summary

- Be the leader your company needs and seek outside help when you need it.
- Have a mission statement that everyone understands (and perhaps to which everyone contributes) and can support.
- Make sure you have job descriptions and procedures in place.
- Maintain a positive attitude so your staff feels you have the confidence necessary to lead them.
- Hire smart and train to make people self-sufficient.

Information taken from a personal interview with Jeff Tempone on November 8, 2010; video © Basso On Business, Inc.

Still Twelve Notes on the Scale

Music publishing executive Evan Lamberg has spent most of his professional life working for such corporate giants as EMI Music. The growth of the Internet—and the changes in music-buying habits that it's brought—have radically altered the music industry since Lamberg first entered it in the early 1990s. And while big industries may have difficulty coping with these changes (arguably, the music industry still seems to be in flux), Lamberg—now executive vice president of creative at Universal Music Publishing Group's East Coast division—has picked up core values in the music field that will always prove valuable. Partially by applying some of the lessons he learned long ago, Lamberg is able to navigate a landscape that is still in flux.

"I don't pine over it," Lamberg says of the way the music business used to run. "It's changing, and it's going to continue to change for a long time. What matters most are songwriters, songs, artists, and producers; *that's* not changing." What matters most, Lamberg says, is the talent. "Yes, there are Internet issues and distribution issues. But you still have to nurture the artist," he notes. Backing up his point, Lamberg continues: "What hasn't changed is there are 12 notes on the scale. Beethoven wrote with the same 12 notes—not a thirteenth note. So the way in which you order those notes, write those lyrics—that hasn't changed. Pop music has the same playing field; that's where it's at. People get free music, and of course, we have to fix that. But if you're not moving people with content quality, they're not going to buy it anyway."

The lessons that Lamberg learned in the early years of his career still apply today. Music has the ability to affect people and even change their behavior; consider the "Hope for Haiti Now" benefit that raised nearly $60 million after the Haitian earthquake in January 2010. The power of music and the talent that drives it remain Lamberg's focus.

Lamberg points to 2010 teen sensation Justin Bieber, whom Lamberg describes as a "15-year-old ultra-talented writer and artist. That's what it's about," he says. "He didn't launch off Disney or *American Idol*. He put his music on the Internet. He's got star power. Everyone around him makes up a solid team. That still works."

Entrepreneurial Insight

Study how your employer embraces innovation, one of the most important ingredients in the business world.

"My Boss Was Chief Lemming"

It's possible to learn from even the people you consider to be the most uninspiring creatures you have ever encountered. For instance, Jeff Hoffman saw a clear example of what is driving down corporations: a dearth of good leadership. He witnessed this firsthand while working in the defense industry. A Yale graduate, Hoffman had a computer science degree with a business minor. "I wanted to be the tech guy with business savvy," he confesses. "I believed that was really the trail."

Hoffman moved to Cape Canaveral to work as an engineer, writing software for launching the space shuttle. "The Department of Defense was doing a lot of work with the Air Force," Hoffman recalls. But his time in the industry seemed less about trailblazing and more Dilbert-like than anything else, he says (referring to the satirical cartoon that highlights the office life of the micromanaged engineer).

"My boss was chief lemming leading us off the cliff," Hoffman says. He recalls a conversation that went something like this:

Boss: Jeff, what do you see?
Hoffman: A parking lot?
Boss: What do you see?
Hoffman: I see cars.
Boss, after a long silence: Every day I look to see whose car is here at the end of the day. Whoever is the last to leave, that person is working the hardest.
Hoffman: Maybe they're inefficient.
Boss: What did you learn?
Hoffman: I'll buy two cars and leave one here.

The boss, a former military man like all the other executives in the company, didn't find Hoffman's suggestion funny. Hoffman decided right then that if this is how individual performance is judged in corporate America, it was not for him. From that day forward, Hoffman became acutely aware of the need to cultivate a culture of real leadership, where those who work *smartly*—not necessarily for the longest hours—reap the greatest rewards. I have mentioned in a previous chapter that I always used to be the first one in and last one out of the office. As a young professional, I was not savvy enough to realize that, if I increased my efficiency, I could produce more impressive results in less time.

Entrepreneurial Insight

Look for what your employer or industry does poorly. Look too for role models who are adapting to change and coming out ahead.

Numbers, Numbers, Numbers

No matter what kind of business you run, it is critical to know your numbers. And I don't mean retaining someone who can explain them to you on occasion. Understand your numbers and, at any given point, you can look at them and see a snapshot of your company and understand in real time the challenges that face you.

Entrepreneurial Insight

Determine the most important focus in your industry that helps to fuel success.

The best training for that may well be at a bank, according to Steve Davies, the former head of US Computer Group, who began his professional life working at Barclays Bank in England. Davies now coaches other entrepreneurs, both through the Alternative Board Long Island and his consultancy firm, Edge Initiatives.

"I went through a great training program from the bank," Davies says. "It's one of the best business training introductions you can have. I received a lot of formal training and a lot of qualifications in economics and law. I know I have a lot more training in business than most people that I run across."

Davies credits his bank training for instilling in him "a key understanding of finance, the interrelations between a balance sheet and profit and loss, which are key performance indicators that allow an owner to understand what's going on in the business." He continues, "A lot of people really don't get a good grounding in that and in operations. Everything is closed out every night for banks; things don't get left over from day to day."

Entrepreneurial Insight

Study good leadership. Does your employer inspire confidence? Hold on to those strategies and be ready to apply them later.

Davies also said he learned from what he considered negatives at the bank—the lack of communication, for example, as well as a pattern of nepotism. These aspects motivated him to become an entrepreneur.

"I wasn't a kid just starting a business," Davies points out. "I was very serious about it." And while computers were not necessarily his passion, Davies recognized the industry's promising potential. "I bought it because I wanted to run a business."

Entrepreneurial Insight

Study bad leadership. Figure out what you can do better in a similar situation.

Mind the Waste

Scott Snibbe, the founder of Snibbe Interactive, spent time working at computer software company Adobe, where he took note of processes and procedures. "I was amazed at the amount of waste produced there," he says. "I couldn't imagine there was so much profit that resources could be so casually taken for granted." And Snibbe wasn't just referring to tangible items like office supplies, electricity, and so on, but human talent as well. At Snibbe Interactive, he looks at his assets differently. "One person does 10 tasks at my company," he explains, adding that firms where the scale is vast "would have 20 people doing the same task."

Snibbe has yet to apply some of these strategies to his firm, but he has these tactics at the ready. "We had a bonus if we shipped at certain times at Adobe," Snibbe explains. "The bonus would decrease every day if we were late. This approach applied some group pressure. I haven't had to institute this policy yet, though it's possible that I might have to at some point." Right now, Snibbe says his employees "hit all our deadlines; but once we're more successful, we can probably offer more of a bonus."

Everything You Need to Know About Risk

Few industries are as ripe with risk as the theater industry, except for perhaps Wall Street. Joe Corcoran has experience in both, working first in downtown Manhattan's financial world, then coproducing *Tony and Tina's Wedding*, and then launching TheaterMania. Despite their apparent differences, Corcoran draws parallels between all of these experiences. "I learned how people think on Wall Street," he notes. Attracting investors, whether for the theater or TheaterMania, means "getting people excited about it, getting people excited with you. Businessmen and Wall Street guys are the investors on these shows. They understand about risk. They can lose it all. We're traveling a journey together, sinking or swimming together."

Knowing how Wall Street operates, Corcoran takes almost the opposite approach when it comes to raising money for theater. "I don't put too much emphasis on the numbers," he says. "It's more like we hope we have a *Jersey Boys* or a *Wicked*, where it takes on a life of its own. If you invest, you can take your grandkids backstage and take pictures with the stars. If it's all about the return, then you probably have the wrong investor, so when they do write a check they understand what good things can happen. The worst that can happen is I can't make money till I pay them back. I'm very fortunate in that respect."

Get Your Framework

> *I learned the framework of how to think about launching a brand.*
> —Selena Cuffe, CEO of Heritage Link Brands,
> about her time working for Procter and Gamble

If you plan to launch a brand, you might as well learn from one of the best. Consider, for example, Selena Cuffe, chief executive of Heritage Link Brands, which imports wines from South Africa and launches them in the United States. Cuffe learned about launching a brand through a previous stint at Procter and Gamble, where she worked on such household names as Pringles and the launch of Tampax Pearl. At Procter and Gamble, Cuffe picked up hands-on experience in successfully establishing a need in a market, demonstrating a value to that market, and more. "I learned the framework of how to think about launching a brand," says Cuffe. "It helped my business acumen."

All of this amounts to powerful tools she now applies to her own business. "When a framework presents itself in my current business, I run with it," Cuffe says.

Entrepreneurial Insight

If you can, work for a big corporation that offers in-depth training in the kinds of skill sets necessary for your industry. Consider such training to be an opportunity to learn while also getting paid.

Learn from the Little Guys, Too

While Barclays, Procter & Gamble, and Adobe may offer powerful lessons, you can't discount the smaller players. It was in this kind of arena, Sandwire founder Adam Schwam claims, where he learned more than he ever did in school. One of his early employers turned out to be a great mentor in the field of promotions, advertising, and old-fashioned entrepreneurship. "He was the brother and friend I always needed," Schwam says. "He was the advice guy, and he went on to launch many companies, including a deli. He and his friends were about 12 years older than I was. I'd watch them open big, explode, and fail, and then pick themselves up. They taught me to see things from beginning to end. I saw him do this, and it made me realize that you can build anything you want." Of course, you can't just build; you need some smarts as well in order to take an idea and turn it into a business. For that reason, Schwam surrounded himself with people who weren't afraid to try, fail, and pick up the pieces.

Entrepreneurial Insight

Recognize the important lessons you can pick up working for even a small player.

You never know where you'll encounter inspiration. So if you're not finding it where you are now, recognize that it's more than likely time to move on. In the meantime, surround yourself with people who are on an active quest to constantly grow, build, and achieve.

What Is Your Yacht?

Each individual has his or her own idea and vision of success. Whether you're a college student, an employee of someone, or trying an endeavor on your own, keep in mind that you are not alone in your pursuit. The people covered in these pages are not dreaming about the life they want to live; they are actively living it. They took their ideas and dreams and turned them into realities.

Take your dream—your yacht, if you will—and make it your own as you carve your path. There is nothing like being your own boss to shape your own blueprint for life. Obviously, not everyone is cut out to be an entrepreneur, so examine your obstacles closely before you decide to do it. Take a look at what's getting in your way, and break down any barriers. If your challenges amount to a need for further education, meeting the right people, or raising funds, then take it from me: There is always a way to break through. But if your heart isn't in it, it's likely not the right path for you.

Whatever your yacht is—financial freedom, more time to spend with your kids, the chance to travel around the world—stake your claim and, just like the people you read about in this book, don't take no for an answer. Jeff Hoffman did not allow a need for additional finances to keep him from going to Yale. Selena Cuffe did not allow her lack of knowledge about wine to prevent her from importing wines from South Africa into the United States. These people have their stories. I have my story. Make your own.

Let your story play out according to *your* rules. May every day bring you closer to a fulfilling and meaningful life.

Summary

While you may be itching to branch out on your own, you don't want to rush this endeavor. There are plenty of lessons to learn first by working for someone else. You will be a stronger entrepreneur by studying the landscape while employed at another place of business. Consider it a live lab where you can pick up tips and strategies to apply later. Here are some suggestions for learning on the job:

- Never mind if you hate your boss. Do your job well, and take note of what your employer does right and also wrong.
- Watch how a business hums. How do staffers make a difference? Analyze whether the manager is effective in keeping operations moving smoothly.
- Recognize how the smart people learn and evolve, ultimately leading to a company's growth.
- Hold on to an industry's core values, no matter how the world around you changes.
- Look for those who can truly lead, and figure out what those who cannot are doing wrong.
- Take advantage of whatever training is available to you. There is no such thing as learning too much.
- Note how your company handles resources, and learn the lessons you can apply in your own endeavor to minimize waste, whether it is in supplies, talent, or time.
- Study how your company motivates staffers and rewards employees for a job well done.
- Pick up what you can about the financial end so that you understand profit and loss, investors, and balance sheets.
- Look at business models, and pick up the best strategies for your own endeavor.
- Learn from the small players too—the folks who try, fail, and pick themselves up and try again.

Entrepreneurial Insights

Introduction

- What do entrepreneurs have in common? The drive to advance. As a rule, this group of people does not let obstacles get in the way of moving forward, whether they need to raise money to get a venture going or they need to educate themselves about an industry, inside and out.

Chapter 1   Lemonade Stands Are Just Too Static

- As an entrepreneur, it may seem as though there are tons of hurdles to overcome. But more than likely you will not overcome any of them without looking risk straight in the eye and moving forward. In a study put out by the Ewing Marion Kauffman Foundation (a Kansas City, Missouri, organization that studies entrepreneurship), 98 percent of those polled said that the biggest barrier to entrepreneurial success was the "lack of willingness or ability to take risks." And there were other barriers, including the time and effort required (93 percent), difficulty raising capital (91 percent), business management skills (89 percent), knowledge about how to start a business (84 percent), industry and market knowledge (83 percent), and family/financial pressures to keep a traditional, steady job (73 percent). Surprising? Not really. No one ever said entrepreneurship was easy. Then again, few things in life that are this satisfying come without difficulty.

- Some entrepreneurs, who grow up watching their parents try to launch a business, learn early on that when there is a will, almost anything is possible.
- This old mantra is true: If you love what you do, "work" becomes that much easier. In fact, it hardly seems like work at all.
- One of the best traits you can have as an entrepreneur is resiliency.
- Enthusiasm coupled with a solid product or service can help an entrepreneur gain entry into almost any marketplace.
- Perhaps the best formula for innovation is creativity, with a healthy dose of conviction.

Chapter 2   Take the Blinders Off

- Entrepreneurs, as a rule, never shrink back, no matter how high the stakes.
- Perceive a demand, and hang in there for as long as the venture proves viable. But that viability is open to interpretation—there is no single magic formula.
- When questioning the rules, suggest a reasonable alternative on which all of the stakeholders can agree.
- Push boundaries, but keep your integrity intact.
- As a business owner, you may work for yourself. But that does not mean you don't have to play nicely with others. Far from it. You need employees, investors, vendors, customers, and prospects to be on your side. So, try to work with the other personalities, no matter how difficult they may sometimes be. Remember: This is in the best interest of your business.
- Keep territories in mind. You do not want to erode your own base.
- Start thinking about your plan B, even if you think you won't need it. This is a good exercise in becoming resourceful.
- Even when you think it is time to fold, take one last look at your assets, since you may still have something of value that the market might want.

- Entrepreneurs see hurdles as doable.
- Rally your supporters. They like to back winners.

Chapter 3 Image and Reputation Matter

- Prepare for the skepticism of prospects, and stay focused on convincing them to take a chance on you.
- Craft your image, but keep it real. Your reputation matters.
- When investors have confidence in you, they may actively seek you out to see how they can back one of your new projects.
- While social media might have begun as a pastime for the young, a growing number of adults rely on these platforms to stay in touch, not just with family and friends but also with colleagues, companies, and customers, according to the Pew Internet & American Life Project. What's more, this group found that people are now "especially attuned to the intricacies of online reputation management," whether they are looking to market themselves or to fly beneath the radar.
- In the age of social media, word spreads fast, perhaps landing you and your company in the limelight—whether you want to be there or not.
- If your website generates comments, do not let them sit. Address them all, even if they are negative.
- Live up to your word. Don't promise anything that will leave stakeholders waiting for you to make good.
- Never be afraid to start at the bottom. This is perhaps one of the most organic ways to build meaningful relationships as you make your way in your industry, whatever it happens to be.
- Effective entrepreneurs know they must be able to lead and plan in order not only to grow a business, but also to inspire faith and trust from others.

Chapter 4 Is That a Leprechaun in Your Pocket, or Are You Just Happy to See Me?

- Create your own luck by positioning yourself in places where good turns happen.

- Don't wait for opportunities, make them happen.
- When the gatekeeper turns you down, ask again if that person knows for sure that the decision maker won't see you.
- A good way to make luck happen: Knock on doors.
- "Luck"—however it's defined—pops up its head when you throw hesitancy aside and ask for that favor.
- When it comes to preparation, go the extra mile. Do one more rep. It will help set you apart from everyone else.
- Build a team of talented and loyal players who can spot a lucky break as it happens and run with the opportunity to make it meaningful for your organization.
- Do business with people you know, and they will think of you first when they come across an opportunity that may give your operation a boost.
- Broadcast your company's good news everywhere. You never know which influencers are paying attention.
- Take the occasional step way outside your comfort zone. You may wind up discovering new and refreshing directions that could help you grow your organization.
- Business award ceremonies are fantastic venues for meeting the real captains of industry in your field.
- Good things happen to those who align their beliefs with their actions.

Chapter 5   Foster Bold Dreams, Bolder Actions

- Want to get noticed? Market yourself to your desired audience, even if they don't expect it.
- If you're big on dreams and short on cash, seek out an investor who has confidence in you. But write a really good business plan first.
- Don't be afraid to make mistakes. Take heart in the fact that you will be better prepared for the next opportunity that comes your way.
- Follow your heart and interests, even if they are way outside the path that you originally expected to take.
- When taking over a family business, don't be afraid to move away from the old guard.

- Less than 33 percent of family businesses survive the transition from first to second generation, according to the US Small Business Administration. And of those that do survive that transition, almost half do not make it through the transition from second to third generation.
- Find the space to nurture and grow your new pursuits.
- Big dreams propel you forward when they are driven by entrepreneurial passion.

Chapter 6   Humble Beginnings

- When first starting out in business, spend as little money as possible, and only on the essentials.
- Travel with the influencers who can help you get to know decision makers.
- In order to create a path for growth, make yourself indispensible in whatever industry you want to be in.
- Understand the needs of your clients so that you can better serve them and as a result earn their loyalty.
- CPAs and other centers of influence make great ambassadors for your brand.
- Train your employees to become good listeners.
- Celebrate wins in a big way. You will attract the best talent to your firm.
- Tell your success stories to the media. Public relations can go a long way toward building buzz in the right circles.
- Observe what other industries are doing well, and adopt those strategies to your own firm.
- Never take your eyes off your most important asset: your customer.
- Team up with partners who have everything to gain by working with you.

Chapter 7   Diving without a Shark Cage

- As a small player, you have to be on top of your game to contend with the big guns.

- Sometimes the best way to compete is to sit back and watch your rivals try something new.
- One of the best and least expensive forms of market research is simply to ask new clients what they liked and did not like about their previous vendor.
- Dropping your prices when the big-box stores encroach can be the worst strategy of all.
- Customer service can be the real differentiator between you and your biggest competitor.
- One of your best assets can be the enthusiasm you bring to the market.
- Put technology—the true equalizer—to work for you in order to compete effectively in the marketplace, even against your largest rivals.
- Once you get a foothold in the market, remember to stay nimble so that you can jump in different directions as needed.
- Venture capital money, if you can get it, may look tempting—but you could wind up losing control of your company.
- Even the best ideas require help, so be sure to get the best support available, whether from a coach or a mentor.

Chapter 8   Fun with Risks

- Most success requires a certain amount of risk, but that doesn't mean you have to lose your shirt.
- Take risks that allow you to maintain a comfortable level of control. Smart risk-taking requires all kinds of calculations and assessments, so do your homework. Plan for the best outcomes, but understand that you may not always meet your goals.
- If you want people to take a risk with you, it helps to have a good track record.
- Risk is often one of the most important ingredients needed to achieve that all-important success.
- Risks may need some fine-tuning. But that doesn't mean you shouldn't take them.
- Successful risk-taking may be the ultimate adrenaline rush in business.

Chapter 9   The Corporate Game

- Working in the corporate world can provide good opportunities to hone your business acumen.
- While working for someone else, try to work in as many job positions as possible so that you can pick up new skills and broaden your network along the way.
- Pick up whatever knowledge you can about business operations while working for someone else.
- Study how your employer embraces innovation, one of the most important ingredients in the business world.
- Look for what your employer or industry does poorly. Look too for role models who are adapting to change and coming out ahead.
- Determine the most important focus in your industry that helps to fuel success.
- Study good leadership. Does your employer inspire confidence? Hold on to those strategies and be ready to apply them later.
- Study bad leadership. Figure out what you can do better in a similar situation.
- If you can, work for a big corporation that offers in-depth training in the kinds of skill sets necessary for your industry. Consider such training to be an opportunity to learn while also getting paid.
- Recognize the important lessons you can pick up working for even a small player.

Afterword

IT'S MORE THAN just a wing and a prayer.

I am on my own journey of sorts—attempting to reinvent myself and use my strengths to benefit others. I have built my entire career by assisting companies and people, and striving to make things better, faster, cheaper, and more reliable. Yet I did not realize how positively I was influencing my clients' lives and businesses. I have always set high goals for myself, creating aspirations that might seem unattainable to some. Still, most of the time, my aspirations come to fruition. Why is that?

From throwing newspapers on porches, to making sandwiches at a deli, to slinging pizza in the air, to running my own companies, I have always had the desire to do—and be—more. From failed enterprises to the creation of BassoOnBusiness.com, I have forged onward to help others with their journey. Helping inspire the entrepreneurial spirit to get America back on its feet and be the catalyst for others to achieve *their* American dream—that's certainly lofty stuff.

Recently, I sat in the makeup chair at Fox Business Network, chatting with the other guests in the green room before I went on air. Suddenly, I was overcome with a wave of emotion. I had been preparing for this moment for many years, and now I was at a turning point. My skills were in synch with my aspirations, culminating in the goal toward which I had been constantly working. No one would have faulted me had I felt nervous; after all, millions of people were about to hear my voice and my opinion. Yet there I was—calm, collected, and ready. My sense of preparedness gave me comfort and incredible satisfaction.

My getting to the green room didn't happen by luck. It was all part of a deliberate plan—one that I'd worked at very hard. And this was just one facet of that overall plan, which—just in the last year—has included meetings with top network executives about upcoming projects and appearances. I made it happen, not by sheer will, but by setting goals and using all the tools and resources at my disposal. My agenda is now filled with speaking engagements and my team is in demand. Things like this don't just happen on a wing and a prayer; the people who *make* them happen work on them happily each and every day.

About the Author

Rob Basso is an *everyday entrepreneur* with a mission—no, a passion—to help small business owners navigate their way to success. Ever since he was in college Rob has been involved in many business ventures, including an ice cream truck route in a highly competitive and contested area of Long Island.

As the owner of the New York region's largest independent payroll processing firm, Advantage Payroll Services (www.liadvantage .com), Rob has interacted with thousands of business owners from virtually all business sectors. With more than 2,000 clients, he has his finger on the pulse of small business and has gained a wealth of knowledge about small business operations and growth. He now shares his insights with start-up business owners, business executives, and entrepreneurs. Recently he cofounded a national bank, and he has also invested in multiple entertainment industry projects. By taking risks and developing creative concepts, he has built a reputation as a successful entrepreneur who is committed to assisting others seek and achieve their American dream.

Rob is the creator of BassoOnBusiness.com, where he shares his experiences and those of other successful business people with a community of aspiring entrepreneurs. The community he has built is focused on inspiring the American entrepreneurial spirit. He has created a destination where business owners can get important tools, strategies, and real world information that is vital to success.

Rob is the executive producer and host of a unique web business video program geared toward helping small business owners to overcome challenges. Each episode is premiered at monthly live events called "Working Lunch with Rob," where Rob helps business owners and professionals work together to fix challenges in their organizations. This empowers and motivates all attendees to implement positive changes in their own organizations.

Rob, a respected small business expert and sought-after speaker, is regularly called upon by regional and national media to comment on issues and trends in small businesses. He is a frequent contributor on *Fox News*, *Fox Business*, and other national news programs. He has been interviewed by *Entrepreneur* and *Time* magazines, and he contributes blogs to American Express OPEN Forum and the *New York Enterprise Report*. He is frequently interviewed by leading newspapers including *Newsday*, the *New York Times*, and *Long Island Business News*. He has appeared in national Associated Press, Forbes.com, MSN.com and Bnet.com articles. He is also a frequent guest on radio programs across the nation and was recently a guest on the *Sean Hannity Show*.

Join the conversation at BassoOnBusiness.com.

Index